D1079343

DEALING WITH DIFFICULT STAFF
IN THE NHS

DEALING WITH DIFFICULT STAFF
IN THE NHS

ROBIN GOURLAY

KOGAN
PAGE

YOURS TO HAVE AND TO HOLD

BUT NOT TO COPY

First published in 1998

Kogan Page Limited
120 Pentonville Road
London N1 9JN

British Library Cataloguing in Publication Data

A CIP record for this book is available from the British Library.

ISBN 0 7494 2370 6

Typeset by JS Typesetting, Wellingborough, Northants
Printed and bound in Great Britain by Clays Ltd St. Ives plc

Contents

Contents

Contents

Acknowledgements

My thanks are due to the many participants at my seminars who have suggested examples of difficult colleagues. I hope that they have all been sufficiently disguised! Also thanks to my daughter Amanda who wrote some of the case studies and to Richard, my son, whose personnel advice was always interesting.

Finally, thanks to Janet, my wife, who has typed innumerable drafts. No one has been difficult – except perhaps me.

Chapter 1

Introduction

Aims and Purpose

In writing this book my aim has been to present a number of approaches to the management of staff whose behaviour is difficult or whose performance is less than adequate.

It is not surprising that there are people in health organizations who are perceived as being difficult. Such organizations employ people from a wide range of professions and disciplines. Many staff see their loyalty as being to their profession rather than the hospital or practice. Professions try to assert themselves by building up the importance of their members so that they are treated as equal rather than subservient. Individual members may react adversely to what they see as an infringement of their clinical autonomy.

Resources are nearly always insufficient and the debate on how to win these can spill over into personal battles and acrimonious relationships. Such wars are then fought in the pages of the media, which is always hungry for a good health story, especially if insensitive and uncaring bureaucrats are apparently ruling the medical and nursing heroes and heroines.

Shortages of money often mean shortages of staff. Many staff are having to work long hours and feel inadequately rewarded for their efforts. They may become bitter towards those whom they see as 'having an easy life', including their own managers.

Expectations of work are changing. People want to have some time for leisure and their families and are not willing to work extremely long hours for the promise of an easier life in later years.

Roles are changing, too. Nurses are taking on more involved medical work, but do not see themselves as being recompensed adequately for this. Sometimes it is not always clear who should do what or whether or not they have been properly trained to fulfil the responsibilities 'allocated' to them.

Patients themselves are more demanding and may become verbally or physically abusive, creating anxiety and alienation in the staff. Their expectations are of high-quality, instant service, such as that which they might receive in the retail world. Such demands stretch the abilities of staff to cope with patients and each other.

Someone once said that hospitals were 'organizations cradled in anxiety'. Being anxious distorts people's everyday behaviour. They can become argumentative, sullen, aggressive, withdrawn, uncooperative, posing great difficulties for those who have to work with them. Fortunately, most staff cope admirably with the sometimes very testing circumstances in which they conduct their working lives, but, occasionally, there is the so-called 'difficult' person.

The approach that has been taken here is to suggest how you can diagnose what causes the difficult behaviour and identify potential levers of change. The importance of defining the outcome you want from your efforts to change the difficult person is stressed and then a series of tools, which you can use singly or in combination to get the results you want, is described.

Like all 'tools' these ones require a little practice before you will find you can use them well, but, from the seminars, it is clear that people can acquire the skills without much difficulty. The success you will have is dependent on your diagnosis of the problems. Sometimes I have found that just showing what the range of problems might be behind the presenting symptoms has been sufficient for a manager to rectify a long-standing set of difficulties they have experienced with an individual.

The Difficult Relationship and its Consequences

'Why are they so difficult? It's obvious what we've got to do – if only they could see sense!'

'Watch out for Dr Smith. If everything is not just as he likes it, he'll blow his top.'
'Mind you, her bark's worse than her bite!'

These comments and observations can be heard many times a day in a busy hospital or GP practice. We wonder why people can't be as reasonable and as considerate as we are – 'If only they were', we sigh, 'we wouldn't have half as many problems and difficulties as we do.'

Hospitals, of course, are not the unique home of difficult people – although this may sometimes seem to be the case. All organizations – even your own family – will contain difficult people at times. Generally, we are able to sort out the difficulties before they threaten the stability or survival of the organization or institution, but not always. In the family, relationships can become too difficult and result in people leaving or becoming violent with each other. In an organization such as a hospital, such syndromes can also happen. The violence may be physical or verbal, but, whatever form it takes, the result is a loss of cooperation and a channelling of energy into unproductive areas where the motive becomes one of getting even or scoring points. Even if the result of difficulty is people 'just doing what they're told – no more, no less', then, again, cooperation is reduced.

Why does this matter? Why are relationships so important? The answer is straightforward. Unless people can cooperate with each other, then the 'product' or 'service' will be endangered. A dramatic and true illustration of this is the story of the staff in the cabin of a commercial airliner. The captain of one airliner was known as a 'difficult' man. He was dictatorial and comments from other crew members were met with a hostile reaction, however well-intentioned the comment was. The consequence? Other crew members only spoke to the captain when he asked them a question. They were afraid of him and fearful of being made to look a fool in the eyes of the other members of the crew.

On one flight, just as they were coming into land, the undercarriage would not lower. The captain took it upon himself to try and sort out the problem. He devoted all his attention to it, oblivious of anything else, while the co-pilot flew the plane.

There was a tense silence on the flight deck as the captain concentrated on the undercarriage problem. No one dared to speak. After a while, the co-pilot and engineer noticed they were getting short of fuel – in fact the level was getting dangerously low. They said nothing in case they incurred the wrath of the still-engrossed captain. Eventually, they crash landed with a number of fatalities. The fuel shortage became so critical that they had insufficient time to plan how to land the disabled aircraft.

What was the cause of this 'accident'? In a technical sense, it was the problem of the undercarriage, but this could have been mitigated had the crew been able to discuss what options were open to them and what considerations they needed to take into account in deciding what to do. However, the 'difficult' behaviour of the captain inhibited this process.

In hospitals, similar 'life and death' decisions are being made. Imagine if the airline captain were a surgeon and that instead of a crew member one of the theatre team observed that an instrument was likely to be left in the patient (it does still happen). If the theatre team member felt unable to point this out for fear of 'having my head bitten off', what would be the consequences for the patient – and ultimately for the surgeon?

In fact, you don't need to imagine such a scenario. In a recent case in the NHS, an allegedly dogmatic and dictatorial pathologist was thought to be 'misreading' slides with the result that patients who were not 'ill' were subject to painful and disfiguring surgery while those who were ill, were missed. The pathologist was allegedly so difficult to deal with that others (including medical staff) 'ignored' the problem, hoping it would go away. It did not, and no doubt many patients suffered considerably as a consequence.

Difficult behaviour does not always, thankfully, result in such dramatic consequences. In my own early days of managing hospitals, my colleagues and I were upgrading a ward. It had been redecorated and the next stage was to put up curtain rails and curtains around the beds. When the newly appointed consultant heard of this, he immediately demanded that we should not do it. We pointed out the privacy it would give to patients and other advantages, but he was adamant, arguing that it would increase infections. Our analysis was that he wanted to make a point to 'management' and that logic was not the way forward. We discussed the problem with some of the 'elder statesmen' consultants who then had a 'quiet word in his ear'. Our objective was to have the curtains and, ideally, gain the cooperation of the new consultant.

This was, in essence, a trivial issue, but it could have soured relationships and inhibited future cooperation if it had not been resolved with no loss of face on either side.

Why is it Difficult to Deal with Difficult People?

Most of us prefer a peaceful life where we get on and do what we have to without interruption. The behaviour of difficult people can inhibit or prevent us from doing what we have or want to do. At the minimum end of the spectrum, their behaviour is a distraction; at the maximum end, it can be physically or mentally abusive. We therefore have to address the difficulties if we are to make progress. This demands our energy, as well as some degree of mental toughness. There are risks in this. We may not be able to get our way and have to back off, we may be made to look foolish, we may not be able to cope with the other's behaviour, we may even risk our jobs, we may upset the difficult person even more or upset others whose cooperation we enjoy or we may not know how to start discussion of the problem. In summary, we become anxious and worried – not a pleasant emotional state to be in. We then ask ourselves if it is worth all the trouble – taking these risks – to deal with the difficult person. After all, we may say, what would happen if it went wrong?

Given these thoughts and emotions, it is not really surprising that we see positive advantages in living with the difficult behaviour, accepting the individual as a difficult person and therefore think that there is not really much we can do about it. We opt for the quiet life. We then excuse our inaction by pointing out that 'they won't listen to reason' or 'they are illogical and irrational'. This we say in our own defence; we believe it because our own approach to problems is – we believe – logical and rational.

This is how we've been brought up and any management course that we've been on has stressed the logical and intellectual aspect of dealing with problems. What we have not developed to the same extent is the ability to handle the 'emotional' aspects of difficult behaviour. I don't mean by this comforting those who break down into tears, although this is one aspect. The emotional aspects cover all those feelings and motivations that lie below the surface of the rational presentation. We need to be able to 'diagnose' these, work out what they are and where their strength lies and then develop approaches to cope.

This demands the apparent paradox of being rational about emotions! This is not always easy. The behaviour of the difficult person will cause emotional reactions in you, so not only do you need to understand the causes of their behaviour, you also need to understand, and perhaps even modify, your own reactions. This does require self-insight and skill in mastering your responses. Given this amalgam of emotions and rationality, compounded in the relationship mix of at least two people, it is not all that surprising that we may not be all that good at dealing with difficult people.

Why are People Difficult?

'If only everyone was like me – balanced, sensible, logical and considerate – there would be no problems.' Of course, no one is like you – and yet everyone is like you! It all depends on how you see and define things. Your tenacity is someone else's obstinacy; your carefulness is someone else's nit-picking.

People can be difficult – or perceived to be difficult – for a wide variety of reasons. In managing or relating to the difficult behaviour, it is essential, as was said earlier, to get below the presenting symptoms. This is what this book sets out to help you to do, and once you have made your diagnosis, you can then decide how to react and behave yourself.

A few illustrations may show what underlies the presenting symptoms and how you might choose to respond. Take the issue of 'territory'. All kinds of disputes between neighbours start off as arguments about where the property boundaries are. One neighbour perceives the other as 'stealing' their property, albeit only a strip 100 m by 10 cm. Because a way can't be found to resolve this difficulty, each of the sides justifies to themselves why they are in the right and the other is in the wrong. They do this by denigrating any aspect of each other that they can. This animosity eventually breaks down the possibility of communication between the parties, at which time war breaks out.

In a health context, you can see such behaviour at work when someone is asked to move office or change some familiar way of working or even losing a member of staff.

A second illustration – and a very powerful one in healthcare – is the differences in what people believe to be right and wrong. An obvious example would be for managers to insist that a devout Catholic should assist at abortions. In this case, management does not appreciate the 'values' of the Catholic member of staff and any refusal on their part could be seen as difficult behaviour by management.

More subtly, there may be differences in perceptions of 'rightness' between doctors and managers. Doctors perceive managers to be bureaucrats whose main purpose appears to be to stop things developing and improving. Managers see doctors as spendthrifts who have little commitment to ensuring the books balance. Each group sees the other as being 'difficult'.

Power battles give rise to our third illustration. Power is about having control. Some medical consultants feel that their GP colleagues are having 'too much control' over what consultants do. I recall a London GP talking to some senior registrars and newly appointed consultants. In his preamble, he commented on this shift in power and how he welcomed it and considered it a good thing that consultants had to pay more attention to GPs. From this relatively harmless remark – said with tongue slightly in cheek – the session nearly degenerated into brawling. People are jealous of their power and its ability to enable them to get things done in the way they would like. Challenge it and you could have some difficult people around.

Motivational issues are also causes of difficult behaviour. An individual produces poor-quality work, is absent too frequently or disturbs other people at work. The causes of such behaviour are legion – one of them may even be you if you are managing this difficult person. I had a colleague who came into the section where I was working. He had a good reputation, but this increasingly came to be seen as ill deserved. Mistakes were made, absences increased; moans whinged round the office. The problem was to do with how he saw his manager – a woman. He saw her as interfering and nit-picking, not allowing him to get on with the job. Of course, she saw him as careless and lazy and, because of this, in need of close and careful management. This increased his feelings of anger and frustration. It became a self-fulfilling prophecy, compounded by the fact that they appeared, superficially, to get on well with each other. However, this masked the real feelings of animosity that they were unable to bring out into the open.

As you will see as you read through the book, there are as many causes and variations of difficult behaviour as there are people who demonstrate them. However, it is possible to 'categorize' the behaviours, making it easier to diagnose causes and develop remedies. People are complicated. Remember, therefore, that dealing with difficult people means getting below the symptoms and addressing the causes of them. This will be a bit like untangling strands of wool that have become twisted together. In the end, though, when all the strands have been separated, you can decide how you want to knit them together to achieve your desired result.

Remember, also, that untangling strands of wool can be very frustrating. If all is not going well, your own hands become sticky with sweat and your patience may wear thin. You get irritable and eventually may throw the whole lot away, arguing that it is not worth the trouble. You will regret this 'opt out', though, if when you go out into the cold, you have no sweater to keep you warm. Outcomes are important; define them and keep them in mind as your untangling proceeds.

Consciousness and Competence

I imagine that you are reading this book because you do not feel as confident as you would wish in dealing with difficult people. As you will discover shortly, you have taken the first step in building both your confidence and competence. Obviously it is difficult, if not impossible, to practise the skills described in this book without some further assistance. If you were attending one of my seminars for health professionals and managers, I would invite you to try out the skills in short, designed exercises with another seminar participant.

To overcome this difficulty, I suggest you work with a colleague you can trust. They can then take on the behaviour of a difficult person of your mutual acquaintance while you practise some of the approaches proposed in the book. At the end of the exercise, your colleague should describe to you how they felt and why they reacted to you in the way they did. You may find that you both find it hard to be serious while you are in the middle of the exercise. Don't worry about this – as the session continues you both can become more serious about it.

Back to the point about you having taken the first step. For many people who need to develop these types of behavioural skills, the first step is actually acknowledging that they don't already possess them. This stage is referred to as 'unconscious incompetence'. This is not meant to be insulting; just an accurate description of the person's status with regard to this set of skills.

The second stage – which is where you probably are – is 'conscious incompetence'. Again, don't take offence; all it means is that you know you can't do it as well as it can be done. Simply by reading this book, you will end up at a higher level of conscious incompetence. If, however, you try out the exercises and follow through the suggestions, you will start moving to the next stage – 'conscious competence'.

In this stage you will feel as though you are behaving unnaturally; which in fact you are because you will be behaving in ways that are different to how you have behaved in the past. You will find yourself having to think deliberately about what you do and how you react to the difficult person. You may even feel as though you are behaving falsely. Don't worry. Remember when you first drove a car? Everything had to be done deliberately and consciously at first, but now you can find yourself at your destination without your ever having been conscious of actually driving there.

This final stage is called 'unconscious competence'. You don't have to think what to do and say next – it all comes naturally. However, to get to this stage, you do need to practise and get some comments on how you are doing. So, try the ideas and skills out and, as you do, your competence will increase. As this increases, so will your confidence.

Chapter 2

Defining the Problem Behaviour

'Early leavers' is a term used to describe those who take up a job and, after a short while, find the work and its content uncongenial and leave.

Early leavers cost money – all the recruitment process has to be gone through a second time; there is a gap that others will have to fill until a replacement is found. Regrettably 'early leavers' are blamed for their inabilities to come to terms with their new job: 'She would never fit in', 'She was a difficult person anyway and it's just as well she didn't stay any longer', 'He upset everyone with his "foreign" ways – I'm glad he's gone'. These are typical of comments made about early leavers. They represent a superficial and defensive view of the problem. We need a much more thorough diagnosis of the 'early leaver' problem.

The Glenda Jones story

Meet Glenda Jones who, as you arrive, is enjoying her first meeting with the ward managers in her surgical directorate. She has recently been appointed to this post after a successful spell as a ward manager herself at a hospital in the North of England. In fact, this is her first move away from the North and she is a little apprehensive about how she will be received.

Glenda has realized that moving South will involve some dislocation to her personal life, but she is ambitious and sees this as one of the inevitable prices to pay for her own development.

Although one of the ward managers at the meeting, Liz Williams, applied for Glenda's job, she has not been appointed, but she appears to hold no grudge about this. In fact, all Glenda's staff (as she now thinks of them) welcome her to the hospital.

Glenda is an enthusiast and, in her earlier tour around the wards, she noticed a number of things she wishes to change. For example, she is a firm advocate of patient care plans and care pathways. She thinks she will sow a few seeds about these at the close of the meeting.

As she mentions these changes, she notices a slight 'stiffening' of the ward managers, but puts this down to their natural resistance to change. She closes the meeting shortly thereafter, mentioning that she will be doing a 'ward round' after lunch. Glenda is a firm believer in 'management by walking about' and is keen to make herself both credible and visible to all staff.

During the following few weeks, Glenda settles herself into her new role. She is having a little difficulty in selling her flat 'up North' and consequently cannot afford to set herself up in her new location. She is living in hospital accommodation during her 'on duty' time and then travelling North to spend her 'off duty' time trying to sell the flat. As she puts it, it is at least an escape from the rather dreary and tatty hospital flat.

She feels that, otherwise, she is settling in well. She has made a number of suggestions to the ward managers on her ward rounds about how to improve the quality of their nursing care.

Initially, she hits it off well with Brian Large, her Clinical Director, and makes a number of proposals to him about how they can improve the directorate. He appears to welcome these and asks her to put them in the directorate's objectives for the coming year. In mentioning these ideas to her ward managers, she meets a little resistance – they are complaining that they are already under pressure with too few nurses. In fact, they ask her to investigate their staffing problems because they are convinced they need more. She discusses this with Brian, who points out to her that their budget is due to be cut even more and so she must maintain the current level of activity with, probably, fewer staff or, perhaps, less skilled, and therefore less expensive, staff.

When Brian then asks her about the ideas and objectives for the directorate, she blows her top. She complains that the ward managers will not do what she wants, and he is no help, just increasing the pressure on her.

After about six months in the new job, Glenda is beginning to wonder if she has made a mistake in coming South. She has made few friends outside work and is becoming disenchanted with her work colleagues. They will not do the most straightforward of things, even though, to her eyes, they make good sense. She has found that her ward rounds are becoming more like skirmishes on a battleground where she feels she has few allies.

She decides to cancel her regular meetings with the ward managers, using the excuse that, if they are so busy, they ought to spend more time actually nursing. Shortly afterwards, she begins to hear complaints from them about not being kept informed and of being left out.

Glenda, herself, finds that she is becoming increasingly busy. Not only does she feel she is running the directorate because Brian Large hardly ever speaks to her, but, in her early enthusiasm, she volunteered for a number of hospital 'working parties' looking at such things as coping with reductions in junior doctors' hours, introducing Total Quality Management and developing her favourite idea of care pathways.

Glenda finds herself going from one meeting to another. This has the advantage that it means she has no time to deal with her increasingly truculent ward managers. They seem congenitally incapable of managing their wards and are always bleeping her. She refuses to answer her bleep now.

It is about seven months since her appointment when the Chief Nurse, Kate Brown, invites Glenda in 'for a chat'. The meeting starts amicably enough, but when Kate mentions the complaints that the ward managers have about Glenda's 'management style', Glenda sees red. She accuses the ward managers of needing to be spoonfed, being incompetent, talking behind her back, spreading gossip about her to Brian Large and so on.

Kate is taken aback by the outburst and counters with the 'fact' that Glenda never seems to be around to help the ward managers with the pressures they have – and, besides, has not submitted the directorate's objectives, which were due in four weeks ago. The argument becomes more heated, until Kate tells Glenda to take a week's leave 'to sort herself out'.

Glenda makes her way to her hospital flat – the dinginess striking her even more forcibly. She longs for someone to talk to.

Meantime, Kate Brown calls in the Director of Personnel to discuss what they should do about Glenda. They review her references from her previous employer, which give no indication that Glenda could be 'difficult'.

They decide that they should gather evidence of Glenda's poor performance with a view to initial counselling and, if this fails, to proceed to disciplinary action.

They do not need to bother. Glenda's resignation is received the next day.

What went wrong?

When you read about Glenda Jones, you can imagine that Kate Brown and the ward managers would have heaved a sigh of relief when they received her resignation. This quite nicely solves a difficult person problem – but does it?

Glenda Jones came from a previous employer with impeccable references. She was a good ward manager and well respected by staff and patients alike. She was ambitious and everyone who knew her saw her as being destined for a senior manager position. Yet, a few months into her job, people were complaining about her; and she was complaining about them. She was becoming prickly and sensitive to criticism. She was unable to persuade other people – particularly the ward managers – to do those things she thought were necessary. She alienated the clinical director. She was unable to get her objectives completed on time. Increasingly, she spent more and more of her time on work that was not directly associated with her job. By all accounts she had little support, but then nobody wanted to support a difficult person. She was probably experiencing some stress at not being able to sell her flat in the North and having to live in – what she thought was – rather dingy hospital accommodation in her new post. Apparently she had difficulty making friends.

Yet, to begin with, there can be little doubting her motivation to do the best for her staff and for her patients. What went wrong? What caused Glenda Jones to become a difficult person?

As you read through the rest of this book, think about Glenda. What is your assessment of the issues and how could preventive action have ensured that she did not resign. Who, if anyone, is at fault?

Behaviour – Rational or Irrational?

At the outset, it is important to realize that everyone's behaviour is completely rational to them. It could be argued that even a schizophrenic's behaviour is rational to them. The problem for us in having to work with, and sometimes manage, difficult people is that of discovering the basis for the rationale of the behaviour that is causing all the problems. It is not a question of whether or not somebody is bad or mad. It is more a question of finding out why they are behaving the way they are and, once we have done this, working out how we can change things for the better.

There may, of course, be reasons for the behaviour that are genuinely outside the scope of our coping abilities. Staff who are suffering the effects of alcohol or substance abuse or who are experiencing serious personal difficulties at home are probably best referred to those professionally qualified to help them. Nevertheless, we can still give them support, however difficult this might be. It is worth noting that stresses in the job can, of course, lead to serious behavioural problems that demonstrate themselves at work and in a person's personal life. It is part of any manager's job to be observant of their staff's behaviour and to note whether or not peculiar behavioural manifestations are occurring and the extent to which the work itself might be a cause.

Causes of difficulties

The above are serious problems, but many of the issues arising in dealings with difficult people are less serious; they are caused by conflicts over work, objectives, resources or needs and interests. Sometimes these conflicts can run quite deeply, such as when they are about values.

Values are those profound beliefs that influence the way in which you behave. For example, you may have observed that there are conflicts sometimes between doctors and managers over the treatment of patients. Doctors whose values are strongly oriented towards doing the best they can for their patients may not accept that resources used in treating them should be limited. Managers, on the other hand – who may have a broader perspective of patients within the community – may believe that what they should be doing is providing the best they can for the majority of the population, even if this means that some, who may need very expensive treatment, have to go without.

Where such conflicting values are strongly held, compromise is not possible. What is possible, however, is a recognition that the values are important and that individual decisions spring from a value system rather than merely from a wish to be awkward or difficult.

Other causes of difficulties may be to do with an individual's motivation and their competence to undertake the work that is required of them. You may consider that Glenda Jones was not managerially competent – although, by all accounts, good at running wards. On the other hand, you might consider that she lacked competence in interpersonal skills, that she rubbed people up the wrong way. So, despite her strong motivation and commitment to patients, her skills in dealing with people and managing a number of wards, you may think, were inadequate.

In trying to work out the causes of problem behaviour, it is important to recognize that it is not always the realities of the situation that cause the difficulties, but, rather, perceptions of that reality. For example, in the past you may have had difficulty with getting craftsmen, such as carpenters and plumbers, to do a piece of work for you. Now, you might generalize from the particular problem, seeing all plumbers and carpenters as incompetent and unable to keep to deadlines. This perception may then influence the way that you deal with a new set of carpenters and plumbers. Thus, you make an assumption that they need to be told precisely what is required of them and chivvied along on every occasion to make sure that they complete the job on time. This process is what we call stereotyping, and it can lead to difficult problems because the relationship is soured from the word go, even though you have had no dealings with this particular group of craftsmen before.

Options

In this book, a range of approaches to dealing with difficult people and their problem behaviours is presented. Whatever approach you take, it is likely to be a little time before you can change the disturbing behaviour. Thus, some of the skills you need in order to handle difficult people are discussed. Many of these skills will deliver almost immediate changes. Other skills are rather longer-term in their execution. For example, it may be that, for a particular individual or group of individuals, you are in a less powerful position than they are to achieve the outcomes you require. This may mean that you need to follow a longer-term approach, building up your own base of power so that you can change their behaviour by means of the sheer power of your own expertise, position or network of colleagues.

Diagnosis and Outcomes

Whatever approach you do take, you need to be clear at the outset what you are trying to do. Maybe it is appropriate in a book oriented towards health professionals to use a medical model to clarify how to work out the causes of problems.

To begin with, you need to undertake a diagnosis of the problem behaviour. This includes an examination of the symptoms and their possible causes. Once you have a reasonably clear view of your diagnosis, the next stage is to be clear about the outcomes that you want. These outcomes will be described in terms of changed behaviour (the establishment of outcomes is discussed later on in this chapter – see page 23).

Now that you have a diagnosis and an idea of the desired outcomes, you can start to speculate as to what action you could take to change the behaviour to achieve the outcomes that you require. The hypothesis you formulate might cover such things as the need to develop the individual's competences, enhance their motivation or, maybe, change the circumstances in which they are working. When you have your hypothesis, you will then be able to generate approaches or options to test whether your hypothesis is correct.

For example, if someone is having major problems in working within a team and always seems to be getting into conflict with team members, you may want to encourage them to join another team to see whether or not the same problems occur in a different setting. If they don't, then you may need to examine the temperaments of the various individuals within the original team that are causing the problems to see how they relate to those of the person you moved. If, on the other hand, even after the move, the person continues to experience problems in teams, then it may be that they need some training in how to work in teams and how to relate more closely to people when trying to solve problems.

You will be able to evaluate the success of your approach as you will have specified your outcomes; you can assess the extent to which they have been achieved.

It is important when trying to deal with difficult people that you are systematic in tackling the issues. Kate Brown was not systematic in tackling Glenda Jones' problems. She leapt in without really doing a diagnosis of the problems that Glenda was experiencing. When Glenda retorted in a fairly heavy fashion, Kate was taken aback and was unable to cope with this properly.

At this stage, you may want to try to diagnose what the problem was with Glenda Jones. Should she be held entirely responsible for what happened? Was she promoted to a post that put her out of her depth? Did her personal problems intrude too much into her working life? Did she try to do too much too fast or were her colleagues 'stick in the muds'? Was it because Glenda was a 'Northerner' moving into a different culture?

If you had been Kate Brown, what outcomes would you have defined to deal with Glenda; and what would you have done?

Diagnosing the causes of behaviour

Julie's story

Julie works on the reception desk in the Out-patients Department. She has been doing the job for about 18 months and generally appears both competent and professional in dealing with patients. However, Mondays always seem to be bad days for Julie. Whereas normally she is quite calm on taking up her position behind the desk, on Mondays she seems harassed and out of sorts. If one of the other receptionists asks her for help, Julie snaps back and says that she has her hands full and 'is having trouble doing her own work, let alone sorting out somebody else's problems'.

People soon learn not to ask favours of Julie on a Monday or even to talk to her until after lunch. Staff jokingly put it down to Julie's heavy weekends, imagining she had some binge from which she needed to recover on the Monday. Because she is normally so pleasant to work with the rest of the week, staff tend to forgive her Monday morning outbursts. However, one particular Monday, Julie is obviously suffering and becoming increasingly anxious and stressed. The papers on her desk seem to be all awry and she starts to snap at patients, accusing them of bothering her unnecessarily. She accuses one patient of being late and then telling lies. This patient complains and the matter is investigated.

It turns out that Julie hates Mondays because these are the days of Mr Hutchinson's clinic, for which she is primarily responsible. Soon after having taken up her job as receptionist, Mr Hutchinson stormed out of the clinic and collared Julie. He accused her of being incompetent, stupid and lazy. Apparently what had gone wrong was that some case notes that should have been at the clinic were nowhere to be found. Julie took the blame for all this, despite the fact that they were eventually found in the junior doctor's sitting-room and had been taken there by Mr Hutchinson's registrar.

Julie, who relies on her salary to keep herself and her daughter together, had, as a result, been very scared of Mr Hutchinson and believes that he might come out again and tear her off a strip, such that she might get the sack. She has not dared to tell anybody of this in case they would then think she is incapable of doing the job and so she has suffered the 'Monday morning blues' ever since the incident.

Julie is not seen as a particularly difficult person generally, but on Mondays she is considered to be impossible. Nobody had done anything about it until her new supervisor was appointed and, noticing Julie's behaviour, applied the diagnostic process described below.

It is easy to jump to conclusions in cases like Julie's. However, if you were a doctor and somebody came to you complaining of chest pains, you wouldn't immediately admit them to theatre for coronary bypass surgery without doing a probing diagnosis first. You might ask when these chest pains occur and when they don't, for example. When the person says that they occur particularly after a heavy meal, you would know that this is probably a problem of indigestion rather than anything more serious. Similarly, in trying to determine the causes of behaviour of people we call 'problem people' it is important to do a thorough diagnosis of the potential causes of such behaviour rather than just assume or act impulsively.

Diagnostic Instrument

1. What are the presenting symptoms of the problem/difficulty? (Describe them in behavioural terms – for example, 'Is antagonistic to colleagues', 'Does not cooperate'.)

  (a) When do these occur/not occur?

  (b) Where do these occur/not occur?

  (c) With whom do these occur/not occur?

2. In your view, what might be the causes of this behaviour(s)?

3. What evidence would support your views?

4. What other causes might there be of this difficult behaviour? (Use the Why? Why? Technique described on page 21.)

5. How would you now define the causes of the difficult behaviour?

Using the Diagnostic instrument

Question 1 The Diagnostic instrument on p.19 is intended to help you to analyse the causes of problem behaviour. Question 1 asks 'What are the presenting symptoms of the problem/difficulty?' It is important that you try to describe these in behavioural terms rather than use terminology such as 'is lazy' or 'obstinate'. If you are able to describe symptoms in behavioural terms it is easier to grapple with the problem than when they are defined rather vaguely. The instrument also asks you to specify when the behaviour occurs and does not occur and, if appropriate, where the behaviour occurs and does not occur and with whom the behaviour occurs and does not occur. These questions will tend to sharpen up your diagnosis and pinpoint areas for further investigation. For example, Julie's behaviour occurred almost exclusively on Monday mornings and not at any other time of the week. Immediately this should have given any astute supervisor a clue as to an area worth investigating. The cause might be a hangover from a weekend binge, but this would be rather unlikely if it happened after every weekend.

So, the next set of diagnostic questions that the supervisor should ask would be to do with what happens on Monday morning in Julie's sphere of responsibility that does not happen on any other day of the week.

Question 2 This is a little more difficult to answer because it asks you to try and identify the causes of the behaviour. To be able to answer this, you will need to be a good observer of behaviour and know something about the history of the person in the job. Alternatively, of course, you could raise the matter with them and, with some of the skills discussed in Chapter 5, The Communication Tool, start to unearth the potential causes of the aberrant behaviour.

Question 3 This question asks you to provide evidence that supports your view for the potential causes of this behaviour. In Julie's case the evidence would be provided if she explained to you the problem that she had experienced with Mr Hutchinson some months ago.

If, on the other hand, you are having to deal with, say, Jim Smith, who is an accounts clerk and constantly missing deadlines, providing rather feeble excuses such as the pressure of work, then you may need to gather a little more evidence to find out the particular causes of this type of problem behaviour. For example, you might find that not only does he miss the deadlines for getting the accounts paid, but his correspondence is weeks behind as well. You might also find that there are complaints from suppliers who are having to chase up their accounts, which are three or four months behind schedule. If you were to look at Jim's desk and find that it is a muddle of files, papers, memos, diaries, accounts and so on, you might come to the conclusion, based on this evidence, that Jim is not very good at organizing himself and that what he requires is help in deciding on priorities and developing systems of work.

Question 4 This part of the diagnostic instrument asks you to probe a little deeper as to the potential causes of the difficult behaviour. For example, if we go back to Jim, you might ask why is Jim so disorganized and why can't he keep to deadlines? In the process of probing further, you might find that everybody comes to Jim and asks him to help them. Jim, being a very kindly person, is always offering support and will put himself out to help someone else – despite the problems this causes for his work. Such probing might also reveal that Jim has strong affiliation needs. He likes to feel a sense of belonging and be liked by people, to a degree that throws out his own work schedule.

By thinking systematically about a 'problem' individual, you can probe beneath the presenting symptoms and can discover the root causes of the difficult behaviour. Obviously it is unwise to probe too deeply. For example, you might ask why Jim has strong affiliation needs and, if you were to have some in-depth discussions with Jim, you might find that he was a neglected child in his family and is now trying to compensate for this neglect. However, this is not our domain and we should be careful not to pry into other people's deeper motives. What we are concerned with is what causes us problems with people while they are at work and what we might be able to do about this. Incidentally, you will notice that we are using the 'Why? Why?' technique in trying to unearth causes of problem behaviour. The Why? Why? technique encourages you to keep asking questions beginning with the word 'why' until you have unearthed the 'real' reason for the behaviour.

With people like Jim, the mere recognition of the fact that they are putting themselves out to try and win friends is often enough of an insight to enable them to organize themselves a little more coherently and say 'no' to people a little more often.

If we apply the diagnostic instrument to a slightly more difficult problem – that of Dr Green – we can see how useful it can be. Dr Green's presenting symptoms are that he refuses to cooperate with his Medical Director in trying to reduce the orthopaedic waiting list, for which he bears some responsibility. He will not accept the Medical Director's authority over him and neither will he accept the need to work more productively. The figures show that his work rate is slower than that of his colleagues while the interventions used are no different. The first series of questions focused on the relationship with the Medical Director and whether or not the antipathy Dr Green feels towards him leads him to behave in such an obstinate and difficult fashion.

If our diagnosis suggests that this is the problem, then it may be that adopting a strategy of using another person to influence Dr Green might be appropriate. If, on the other hand, it is not this, then the second question comes into play, which enquires about the causes of the behaviour. For Dr Green, you might propose that the cause of his behaviour is an unwillingness to accept that he is not autonomous and the sole determiner of his own workload. In other words, he is not going to accept the authority of anyone else. You might then gather evidence to see whether or not this view is supported in other areas. Does Dr Green accept the pressure exerted on him from his peers, for example? Has he always been reluctant in the past to do what has been asked of him, preferring his own counsel?

If we now apply question 4, which is to do with what other causes there might be of this difficult behaviour, we could ask why is Dr Green like this? We may find that he believes in the traditional authority of the consultant and fears that any erosion of this might be the thin end of the wedge and lead to managers questioning how he practises orthopaedic surgery.

Question 5   Continuing with the analysis of the case of Dr Green, when we come to question 5, we might summarize the causes of the difficult behaviour as something to do with a fear of losing autonomy and maybe even self-respect, coupled with a fear of others telling him what to do. Such a diagnosis could then lead to adopting an approach based on assuring Dr Green of his autonomy and maybe even negotiating a deal with him that reinforces this and also enables the medical director to achieve what he requires in terms of Dr Green's waiting list.

In summary, therefore, just as in medicine, undertaking a proper diagnosis starts to enable us to identify the causes of the problem and the causes of those causes of the problem. Once we have done this, we will have a better understanding of the dimensions of the difficult behaviour we are dealing with, which will enable us to select the right approach, tool or technique to change the behaviour. If you don't do a proper diagnosis, then you will end up using the following tools and techniques in a splatter gun approach, hoping that something will 'stick'. This clearly is a waste of time and effort when a little preliminary thinking and diagnostic work will enable us to target the behaviours more precisely.

Defining outcomes

We now come to a consideration of the nature of outcomes.

You have carried out a diagnosis of your difficult person, defined the problems they are causing you and teased out the possible reasons for their behaviour. Your next step is to consider the ways in which you want them to change. Just as working on the diagnosis was important to understanding your difficult person, so it is important to spend a little time thinking through the outcomes that you are going to try and achieve from your efforts to change them. If you do not do this, then it will be like aiming for a target that is in the dark.

Tom Brown's lab days

Tom Brown is a medical laboratory assistant who does technically competent work – his results are always accurate and produced on time. However, he irritates other members of the laboratory by his exhibitionism – particularly in meetings, when he boasts of not only his technical success, but also his success with members of the opposite sex. Initially, his colleagues took this as youthful enthusiasm, but they have become more and more tired and frustrated with Tom and his behaviour. So much so that they are now refusing to attend meetings at which he is present. As these meetings are important – because they address issues of quality in the laboratory – it is essential that everyone is there and takes a full part in the meeting.

Tom's boss, Fred Sharpe, has had a word with him in the past about his behaviour, but to little effect. Unless things improve there will continue to be extremely bad feeling in the laboratory, with the possibility that overall performance will drop.

Fred has decided to have another go at remedying the situation. He has undertaken a diagnosis in the way discussed earlier and is now trying to formulate some outcomes relating to the changes that he wants to see in Tom's behaviour.

In setting about defining these outcomes, Fred is using the acronym 'BEST', which stands for *b*ehavioural, *e*xpressed positively, *s*pecific and with a *t*ime horizon. Obviously, outcomes have to be expressed behaviourally because when dealing with difficult people it is their behaviour that you are wanting to change.

Outcomes should be expressed positively because this will indicate what you want the person to do, rather than stop doing, moving things forwards. When it comes to evaluating the success of your change efforts in terms of the outcome, it is easier to identify those things that are being done positively rather than those things that are no longer being done.

The outcome needs to be specific and not a catch-all phrase such as 'be better with people'. You have to turn this into something much more precise so that you can define the exact behaviours you want the other person to demonstrate so that they will be better with people.

Finally, it is sometimes an idea to put a time horizon to a change effort. Changing someone's behaviour normally takes a little while – although it happened very fast on the road to Damascus in Biblical times! Such rapid change is rare, and when dealing with difficult people you will probably need to take a number of steps to bring about the requisite changes in their behaviour.

Thinking about the elements of the acronym, Fred has decided that he wants Tom to behave in a way that engenders the cooperation of others. Specifically, he wants Tom to listen more carefully to what others are saying and control his own contribution so that it fits into the context of the discussion. He also wants Tom to ask questions of the others to draw out from them what their views are and the reasons for those views. Further, he wants Tom to be more helpful to the others because, undoubtedly, he is very competent technically. He wants Tom to offer help and assistance to those who are less competent than he is and may be having difficulties in completing their work. Fred is going to start working on Tom in ways that we will discuss later, and he expects that within two months there will be changes in Tom's behaviour at meetings and in the laboratory.

In summary, Fred has identified the following outcomes that he wants to achieve:

- he wants Tom to listen to others and ask them questions to draw out their views
- he hopes to persuade Tom to offer help to others so that everyone can get their work completed on time
- Fred hopes that, by providing feedback to him, Tom will gain some insight into the way his behaviour impacts other people; Fred hopes to achieve these changes within two months.

By defining the outcomes in this way, Fred can now determine what sort of approach might be useful to achieve the requisite changes in Tom's behaviour. If he had not done this, he may well have decided that what he wants is for Tom to be more cooperative but be unsure what this actually requires in terms of specific behaviours. He might also have said that he wants Tom not to boast, but instead he has expressed this positively by aiming to channel Tom's energies into helping other people who are not as technically competent as he is.

The next step for Fred is to consider how he might evaluate the success, or otherwise, of his strategy. There are three aspects that he can use for this evaluation.

First, he can specify what he hopes to see happening in the laboratory once Tom's behaviour has changed. For example, he is expecting to see Tom working with colleagues in small teams on various analyses. He is also expecting to see Tom take his place at meetings with everyone else sitting round the table, discussing ways of improving the quality of their service.

Second, Fred considers what he might hear once his change efforts have been successful. In this case he anticipates hearing complimentary remarks about Tom from his colleagues and hearing from Tom what satisfaction he is getting from helping other people with their particular workloads.

Third, Fred is considering how he might feel once Tom's behaviour has changed. At the moment he feels very uptight at meetings with Tom and gets increasingly angry and frustrated at Tom's boastfulness. Fred reckons that at future meetings he will feel more relaxed and content with the progress being made if Tom's behaviour changes.

Using these three aspects for evaluating Tom's changed behaviour, Fred can assess how well his change strategy is progressing.

The Outcomes questionnaire below is one that you can use to specify your desired outcomes and detail the evaluative criteria of see, hear and feel. As an exercise, you might like to consider the outcomes you would like to achieve if you were managing Glenda Jones and her problems.

Outcomes

1. What outcomes do you wish to achieve in your change efforts? Are they behavioural, expressed positively, specific and with a time horizon?

2. What will you see if the outcomes are achieved?

3. What will you hear if the outcomes are achieved?

4. What will you feel if the outcomes are achieved?

We will refer to outcomes again when we talk about the levers of change, but, for the moment, let us stress how important it is to be clear about the outcomes you would like to achieve in dealing with your difficult person. When you have completed a thorough diagnosis and defined the desired outcomes, you will be in a much better position to decide what approach to take to bring about the changes in the person's behaviour. If neither of these has been done properly, you will just be 'shooting in the dark'. You may hit the 'target', but it will be more through happenstance than would be the case if there had been clear analysis, thoughtful preparation and deliberate efforts.

Chapter 3

Levers of Change

First of all, a definition. 'Levers of change' are those forces that impact on an individual such that if their potency were altered they would affect the behaviour of that individual. The forces can be either real or perceived.

The underlying rationale relating to the levers of change is based on the concept of force field analysis. This proposes that anybody's attitude or behaviour is, at any one point in time, in a state of 'dynamic equilibrium'. That is to say, it is as it is because there is a bundle of forces pushing it in one direction and an equal bundle of forces restraining it from moving in that direction. These two forces counterbalance each other. Therefore, a person's behaviour is a consequence of the interaction of these forces. Should you wish to try and change someone's behaviour, then the logic is that one set or other of the forces has to change its potency.

The case of Frank Pink

Take the case of Frank Pink, who is a hospital porter assigned to do a variety of jobs throughout the hospital. Frank is difficult. If you ask him to do anything he turns disagreeable and generally displays considerable unwillingness to do what you ask. The consequence is, of course, that nobody ever asks him to do anything, which gives Frank an easy life. The strange thing about Frank is that, in his spare time, he works for a charitable organization where he is accepted to be a most congenial companion who will lend anybody a hand.

Frank's behaviour at work is a puzzle to the Head Porter, Joe Barry. Daily, Joe gets complaints about Frank's behaviour and his unwillingness to undertake any 'extra' work. It is getting to the stage where Joe begins to think that he will have to get rid of Frank because he is creating such a bad image for the portering service as a whole.

However, Joe has decided to undertake a diagnosis of Frank and define the outcomes that he wants to achieve. These are that Frank will willingly accept requests from other members of staff and show willing to do the odd jobs that are required of him. Joe sharpens these outcomes further and also specifies his evaluation criteria in terms of what he wants to see, hear and feel when Frank changes. Joe also carries out a force field analysis on Frank. He identifies those forces that will drive Frank to adopt the outcomes that he – Joe – wants and those forces that restrain Frank from creating these outcomes.

On the driving forces side of a force field analysis diagram (see Figure 3.1, page 30), he puts down that Frank:

- likes to be liked
- has a commitment to people less fortunate than himself
- generally seems to enjoy his job
- will do a good job when committed to it.

Turning to an analysis of the restraining forces that are preventing Frank from moving towards the outcome, Joe has a little more difficulty. He proposes the following:

- too many bosses, resulting in his being given a variety of instructions
- no clear job
- being at everyone's beck and call
- being treated as a skivvy
- not achieving job satisfaction.

Joe, as is suggested later, then does an analysis of the potency of these forces and decides that if he can create a job that makes Frank feel that he is genuinely wanted, not just a slave to everyone, he will probably be able to change Frank's rather disagreeable behaviour. To do this, Joe assigns Frank to one of the busiest departments – Accident, Emergency and Out-patients – and indicates to

Frank that this is his territory and that he will report to the Out-patients Manager on a daily basis regarding the work to be done.

Frank initially seems a little reluctant to accept this, but moves into the redesigned job. After an initial settling in period and once he got to know people, he has become an extremely valuable member of the team.

What Joe has done is to recognize that Frank needs to have a much greater sense of belonging than perhaps most people do, and a clear set of responsibilities for which he is accountable to only one or two people, rather than a whole host. Joe has identified the levers for change and 'calculated' their potency. By changing the restraining forces and their potency, he has created a shift in Frank's attitudes to work. His need for structure and affiliation are the forces Joe adjusted, which have enabled Frank to develop greater job satisfaction and, thereby, become a respected and valued member of the department – and, of course, no longer a difficult person.

Defining the 'Forces'

Joe's is a brief and straightforward description of the levers of change method of analysis.

For the people you have to deal with, it is important to be comprehensive and accurate in identifying the various levers. First, though, bear in mind that the forces of change are those that will move the individual to the outcomes that you are trying to achieve. So, the driving forces are those that will drive the individual towards your defined outcomes, while restraining forces are those forces that will inhibit or restrain the individual towards your outcomes.

Once you have identified the forces, it will be obvious to you that not all of them carry the same potency or power to affect the individual's behaviour. It is ideal, therefore, if you can indicate the relative potencies of the forces so you know the ones that are going to give you the most leverage should you be able to work on them successfully. You may wish to score the potencies on a scale of, say, 1–10, with 10 being the most potent.

There is an important wrinkle to using the levers of change method, and it is that it is better to try and reduce the effect of the restraining forces than increase the effect of the driving forces. If

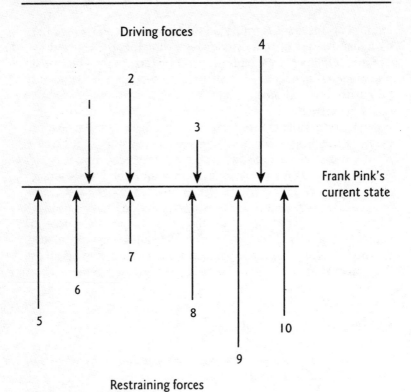

Figure 3.1 Joe Barry's analysis of the levers of change for Frank Pink's behaviour

Key:

Driving forces

1	Likes to be liked	Potency 6
2	Wants to do a good job	Potency 7
3	Respects the hospital	Potency 2
4	Commitment to less fortunate people	Potency 8

Restraining forces

5	Too many bosses	Potency 5
6	No clear job	Potency 5
7	Feels like a skivvy	Potency 3
8	No job satisfaction	Potency 6
9	Not feeling part of a team	Potency 8
10	No long-term relationship with patients	Potency 7

you think about it, one of the forces that could drive a smoker to give up smoking is the health education publicity about the damage that smoking does to your health. On the other hand, one of the restraining forces that makes it difficult for the smoker to give up is their addiction to nicotine. It is far better to try to reduce the addiction to nicotine by some process or another than it is to keep on stating the positive health message of smoking being injurious to your health, however powerfully you do this.

Thus, when you are dealing with your difficult person and analysing the forces after you have assessed their various potencies, your first point of attack should be to try and reduce those restraining forces that are of maximum potency.

Discovering the 'Forces'

One of the difficulties of force field analysis – and therefore of identifying the levers of change – is to know with reasonable accuracy what the forces are that are playing on the individual, whether they be driving or restraining forces. If you are working with an individual who recognizes the problems that they are causing themselves and is committed to change, then it is relatively easy to discuss with them what they see as being the driving forces and restraining forces that impact on their behaviour. However, when you are dealing with difficult people who may not even have an insight into the causes of their difficulty or the fact that they are being difficult, then your only option for ascertaining the nature and potency of these forces is to observe them and have oblique conversations with them.

Clearly, you can't go out to a Frank Pink and ask him what it is that is driving him to be disagreeable and what it is that is restraining him from being agreeable. If you were to do this, you might get a not-so-polite brush-off. However, you could, perhaps, raise the discussion obliquely with such a person and ask how they find the job, what is satisfying about the job and what is not so satisfying. If you know that the individual is involved in outside work in another capacity, you might ask them to draw a distinction between the two types of work and identify what they prefer about one compared with the other.

You do need to be careful how you do this, though, as if the individual 'gets wind' of the fact that you are going to try and 'change' them then, quite naturally, they will be offended and possibly become even more resistant to change. People do not like to be manipulated.

So, we are left with observation, oblique conversation and, perhaps, discussion with the person's colleagues to find out what the forces are. It may be that, eventually, you build up such a relationship with the individual concerned that you can bring the question up more directly – particularly if you employ some of the rapport-building tools that are talked about in Chapter 6. However, for the moment, all that you can hope to be is systematic and as objective as possible, recognizing that your analysis may initially be inadequate. However, doing the analysis can lead you to think about some of the tools that you might employ to achieve the outcomes that you want. For example, if, as we have already mentioned, you do find it difficult to identify which forces are at work, then you may want to bring in to play rapport-building tools earlier on so that you can discuss with the individual, in a more open fashion, the difficulties that they are having in performing the job to the requisite standards.

Using the Levers of Change Worksheet and the Force Field Analysis Instrument

Begin by using the levers of change worksheet (see page 33) to define the outcomes you wish for. Then, turn to the force field analysis instrument (see page 34) to analyse the driving and restraining forces and their potencies. Record the Levers of change worksheet. Then, using the force field analysis action plan (see page 35), decide what specific actions you are going to take to reduce the potency of the top three restraining forces, and increase the potency of the top two driving forces.

Levers of change worksheet

1. Specify the outcomes you want in the future.

2. Specify those forces that impact the individual, driving them in the direction of the requisite changes.

3. Specify the potency of those forces, with 1 being of little potency and 10 having the most potency.

4. Specify the forces that inhibit or restrain the individual from moving in the direction of the requisite changes, then specify their potencies.

5. Specify what actions you could take to reduce the potency of the restraining forces and increase the potency of the driving forces, starting with those with the highest and lowest potencies respectively.

The purpose of identifying the levers of change is to guide you to the tools that you might need to use. As you understand more and more about the causes of the difficult behaviour and the forces that are impacting on an individual, you may find you need to revisit the levers of change worksheet to look at the respective potencies. In particular, when you are trying out some of the tools, you may find that they are not as effective as you would wish. You may therefore want to look at the worksheet again to see whether or not there are any that you might have missed in your initial analysis. Don't forget that we are dealing with a very complicated set of matters – namely, the behaviour of a human being – and it would be irresponsible to believe that it is just a simple matter of changing one or two forces that affect a person and thereby you achieve the outcomes you want. Human behaviour is often very complicated with a great number of intertwining variables. In our analysis, we

Force field analysis instrument

No.	Driving forces	Potency	No.	Restraining forces	Potency

Force field analysis action plan

No.	Action to be taken

can try to highlight some of these and work on them to see what effect this has. As we increase our understanding of the other person, we can revisit the analysis and, perhaps, try a different set of tools and techniques to bring about the required changes as necessary.

In the next chapter, the tools used to effect change are introduced.

Chapter 4

Tools and Techniques for Change

On Being Genuine

The change techniques and tools that you use will depend on your analysis of the causes of the problem behaviour, the outcomes you are trying to achieve and the forces playing on the difficult person. Ideally, what you are searching for is a commitment to the changes as specified in the outcomes you have decided on. This is not always possible, and you may have to do with second best, which you might describe as a compliance to the change. That is to say, the problem person is willing to go along with a new set of behaviours without really committing themselves absolutely to them. There is, of course, the ultimate tool (which will be described fully later), namely the removal of the person from the job. It must be stressed that this is the ultimate tool and that there are many other approaches that are worth trying to gain the commitment or the compliance of the individual to the changed behaviours that you require. Another small word of warning is that some of the tools really are quite powerful. For example, the tool for building rapport with someone can have quite an effect on the person concerned.

In using these types of tools, it is essential that you are clear about your own motives. It is very easy to manipulate people using these tools. You must therefore be genuine in your use of them, implementing them because you want to achieve the outcomes that you have specified, which will make things better for you, your people and for the hospital or other organization itself.

Any attempt to use the tools to further your own personal ends is likely to result in failure when this is discovered. People will find you out and will not trust you in the future, creating resistance to change. Even the power tool (see page 110), which has as its objective achieving compliance from the other person, can be misused. As is pointed out when discussing the power tool, unless you use power with integrity, it will backfire on you. That is to say, people will detect that your use of power is to play games with them. They will find their own way of getting their own back or isolate you by building up their own bases of power.

So, the message is to be authentic in your use of the tools and to genuinely want to use them to improve the relationship for the betterment of the other person, yourself and the organization.

Finally, before we get on to describing the tools proper, it must be pointed out that a single tool may be insufficient to achieve the outcomes that you are after. Many of the tools are best used in combination with each other. A good example is the communication tool (see page 40). Where there is ineffective communication between you and the problem person, it is unlikely that some of the other tools will work successfully.

Another example is the rapport-building tool (see page 49), which needs to be used in combination with a discussion of values (see page 104). Recognizing the differences between your own and the other individual's values and yet being able to live with these differences is part of getting along.

Another combination that is quite frequently used is the power tool together with the negotiation tool (see page 89). With this pair of tools, you are building up a base of power for yourself that then gives you strength for the negotiation. As you will see when you read about the negotiation tool, negotiation is not seen as a process where you squash the opposition or the other party, but more one where two parties of equal strength negotiate a deal that meets the requirements of each.

As has been said earlier, and cannot be stressed too often, human behaviour is a very complicated mixture of factors. These can have many causes and it would be simplistic to think that a single approach based on the use of a particular tool will deliver the outcomes you seek.

In summary, therefore, your selection of tools will be dependent on your diagnosis, specification of outcomes and the levers of change that you see driving or restraining the problem person from behaving as you would like. It is the levers of change especially that will give you a clue as to which is the most appropriate tool or combination of tools to use. Just as you have been careful and thorough in your diagnosis of the causes of the behavioural problems and also analytical about the outcomes you are after, so you must plan carefully how you will deploy the various tools. For you to suddenly demonstrate a new set of behaviours on your part will only arouse suspicion. The problem person will wonder what book you have just read or what course you have just been on and their resistance will be heightened to any attempts you make to achieve your desired outcomes. So, plan your approach carefully, step by step, making sure that your behaviour is genuine, congruent and consistent.

Remember, too, that we are talking about skills in the use of the tools and so you can apply some of the tools to individuals who are not necessarily problem people, even members of your own family. This enables you to practise using some of the tools. This particularly applies to such skills as paraphrasing, which is part of the rapport-building tool.

Chapter 5

The Communication Tool

The communication tool is the most fundamental of all tools. With the possible exception of the confrontation tool (see page 59), all the others require you to involve yourself in two-way communication with the problem person. The emphasis, often, when talking about communication is on sending messages to the other person. With this tool, however, implicit in it is the belief that the most powerful element of communication is your skill at listening to what the other person has to say. When we discuss the rapport-building tool (see page 49), you will see how important the skills of listening really are.

A problem is that difficult people are often rather difficult to listen to because you are in conflict with them, you are unhappy with them or you are disgruntled with them. All these feelings can get in the way of you hearing what they are saying and genuinely wanting to hear what they say. The feeling is that you have heard it all before and that all they do is moan and whinge at you.

The communication tool will help you get through these rather negative processes and move to a more positive basis for discussion where you listen carefully to what they are saying and, eventually, by means of your rapport-building skills, encourage them to listen carefully to what you are saying.

However, let us consider what the problems are when you are communicating with another person and experiencing some difficulties. If you think about it, when another person sends you a message, that message is interpreted by your brain in the context of a variety of situations that you have experienced in the past. You therefore filter or distort the message in some way or another, quite unconsciously. In the context of difficult people, perhaps the most significant filter is that of defensiveness, both on your part and that of the difficult person.

Defensiveness – Beware

What is defensiveness? The defensive filter is one that you erect around yourself to explain away any potential criticisms that the other may be making of you and, of course, the other person does likewise. So, if the difficult person says to you that your style of management needles them because you are always supervising them so closely that they never have any scope to do the things they think right, you may react defensively. You may say to them that of course you do that because they have shown in the past that they cannot be trusted to do the work properly. In other words, you reject the criticism as being any fault of yours and turn it into an attack on the other. You can just imagine how the discussion might then go.

In dealing with the defensive filter, I am not saying that you accept all the criticisms that are levelled at you by the other person. Rather, I am suggesting that you acknowledge that there are genuine concerns the other person has about you and that you be willing to discuss these, searching for understanding rather than rationalization. By this is meant that you try to see whatever the difficulties are from their perspective, not just your own. And, of course, you need to encourage the other person to do the same. You may even ask them how they think you and others react to their 'behaviour'. However, do not say 'don't be defensive' because this is almost an open invitation for them to be defensive; they believe they have every right to be defensive.

The skill in overcoming defensiveness is in asking the other questions to encourage them to analyse the consequences of their own behaviour.

Assumptions

Another filter that you might come across is based on 'assumptions', which is where you assume that the other person should be doing certain things and they assume that they should not be.

Sally Jones and the washing-up

On the ward, the nurses assume that Sally Jones – the domestic assistant – should be doing all the washing-up and clearing away after the patients have had their tea. Sally Jones, on the other hand, assumes that once she has served the tea she can then go off duty as she has worked the requisite number of hours for that particular shift.

The nurses are always chastising Sally for sloping off early and not finishing off her job. Sally takes this badly and, in her turn, accuses the nurses of being slovenly and leaving all the washing-up for her to do the following morning. Their arguments can become quite abusive, with accusations and counter-accusations.

The relationship sours so that if the nurses ask Sally to do any particular favours for them or any small task that is outside the scope of her job description, Sally refuses. Sally has thus come to be known as an obstinate and difficult person.

What really needs to be done here is for both parties to check out their assumptions against what Sally is actually required to do, and what the nurses expect her to do. This may mean a change in the nature of Sally's job, a reorganization of duties or, possibly, the nurses accepting that it is not Sally's job to do the washing-up and tidying away.

Stereotyping

Another potential cause of friction between people is stereotyping. An example is the case of Bill Brown.

Bill Brown – a stereotype?

Bill Brown is a plumber by training, but can turn his hand to most things. He works for the Works Department, which has an unsavoury reputation in the hospital. Unfortunately, all the staff that work for the Department have been tarred with the same brush so that whenever Bill is asked to do a job of work within a ward or department, the staff there stereotype Bill as being a member of the Works Department and, therefore, think he will be lazy, inconsiderate and unwilling to do more than is strictly necessary.

When Bill goes to a ward or department to do a job, he is greeted with animosity and an expectation that he will do the minimum to get by. Bill, on the other hand, in his heart of hearts would like to do a good job, but the staff are so belligerent towards him that he asks himself why should he put any effort into the job when everyone is so unpleasant to him? This becomes a self-fulfilling prophecy because Bill behaves in a way that the others expect. Bill, and all his mates in the Works Department, become problem people.

Stereotyping is very pervasive in our culture. For example, generally, those in the South of England tend to think of people who come from the North of England as being rather slow, dull and obstinate and perhaps a little fond of cricket and beer. Whereas this may be true of a very, very small proportion of northerners, it certainly isn't true of the majority. Yet, if you are a southerner, should somebody speak to you with a northern accent you might immediately jump to the conclusion that they are slow, dull, obstinate and so on and treat them as if they are.

The important message here is that, when dealing with this particular filter, it is vital to accept an individual as they are and check out the preconceptions you might have before you make any judgements about them.

How to Listen

There are one or two things that you can do that will improve your listening skills and reduce the effect of some of these filters.

For example, are you the sort of person who tends to finish off other people's sentences? If you are, be patient and let them finish the sentence themselves. Another thing that many people do is to make up the answer to the point being made by the other person before the other has actually finished speaking. While they are developing their answer, they are not actually listening to the points being made by the other and may, therefore, miss some aspect that is of crucial importance in dealing with the difficulties. Another good discipline is to determine that you will reply to the various points they make one by one after they have finished speaking. Sometimes it is useful making a mental note of the number of points which they do make so that you can reply to them. Another good tip is to ask questions of the other to draw out from them the points that you were not too clear about. In this way you clarify your understanding of what it is that they are saying before you make the points that you want to make in reply.

These are significant communication techniques that will enhance your understanding of others. It is difficult to use these when dealing with difficult people because such people tend to arouse frustration and irritation in you and make you want to get your point across to them without really listening to the points that they want to make to you. For example, if you watch two people who are in conflict with each other or having a general disagreement, it is often the case that they are talking on two parallel wavelengths, and, as we know, parallel lines never meet. It is as though there are two quite separate conversations going on at once. What is needed is an approach to bring at least one of the parties onto the same wavelength as the other. A good technique to use in this case is that of 'paraphrasing', which will be described a little later (see page 50).

'Hidden Messages'

A problem in communicating with people, especially those who are difficult or cause us problems, is the fact that we sometimes send more than one message at the same time. For example, imagine that a slightly bossy staff nurse is talking to a junior nurse she thinks is not doing the job quite as well as it should be done. The staff nurse says to the junior nurse, 'Let me help you with that'. The junior nurse responds by refusing the offer of help, which she sees as an attempt by the staff nurse to take over the job and instruct her on how to do it. In other words, the junior nurse detects a second message, which is that she is not sufficiently competent to do the job properly. Naturally, she takes this as an insult and refuses the offer of help.

The staff nurse, of course, also feels aggrieved because she can quite properly say that all she was offering was her help. However if we delve a little deeper, we may find that she did want to interfere and take over the job from the junior nurse because she thinks she is incompetent. These sorts of communication problems are really quite difficult to disentangle. What one needs to do is be able to build up a relationship of trust so that individuals can explore how communications impact on each other in the relationship. This is where Johari's window comes into its own.

Johari's Window

You can see an example of a Johari's window in Figure 5.1. 'Johari', incidentally, comes from the two Americans Jo Luft and Harry Ingham who put their names together to give their interesting way of looking at relationships between people a name. What they have pointed out is that there are behaviours and attitudes you have that are known to you and are also known to others. This is the 'open self'. There are also views and attitudes you have that you keep concealed and are not known to others. This is box 2 in Figure 5.1 – the 'concealed self'.

Equally, other people have attitudes towards you and thoughts about you to which you are blind but which they know about. This is box 3 – the 'blind self'. Then there is an area that is hidden from both you and others. It may be, for example, that you have hidden motivations or abilities that circumstances or events have not brought to the fore. At the moment, you and others are unaware of them. These aspects make up the 'unknown self'.

The idea behind Johari's window is that if we can create more openness between people then the likelihood is that there will be fewer problems in communications and so fewer problems in relationships. In other words, it is suggested that we need to have more of our behaviour and attitudes in the 'open self' part than in the 'unknown self' part. If you look at Figure 5.2, you will see how Johari's window can be used to show an interaction between our staff nurse and junior nurse. The staff nurse is quite open in commenting on her offer of help to the junior nurse. The junior nurse, as mentioned, picks up a double message and initially refuses the offer of help. However, suppose she were to take another

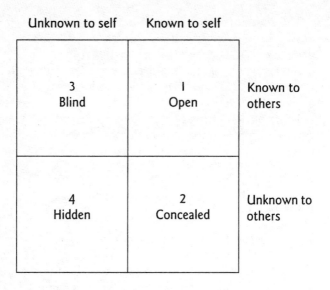

	Unknown to self	Known to self	
Known to others	3 Blind	1 Open	
Unknown to others	4 Hidden	2 Concealed	

Figure 5.1 Johari's window

approach and say to the staff nurse something along the following lines:

> 'Staff nurse, I appreciate your offer of help and would like to take advantage of it, but it seems to me that you do not think I'm competent to do the job and that you really want to take the job from me. This upsets me.'

This is response 1 in Figure 5.2. You will note from the figure that the junior nurse is thus feeding some information from her concealed self to the staff nurse's blind self. This opens this area up a little as, before the junior nurse's response, she was unaware of the impact of her communication on the junior nurse.

The problem comes now. Should the staff nurse react defensively to this communication from the junior nurse and deny the hidden message. If she does, then there are some problems with such a move. However, let us assume that she reacts in an equally open fashion and says to the junior nurse something along the following lines:

> 'You are right, I am concerned about your abilities and I felt that I could do it better, but I am sorry you are upset.'

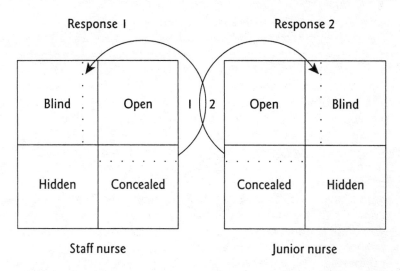

Figure 5.2 Using Johari's window to analyse the conversation between the staff nurse and junior nurse

The staff nurse is now feeding some information from her 'concealed self' through to the junior nurse's 'blind self' (see response 2 in Figure 5.2). The junior nurse may have had a feeling that this was what the staff nurse was thinking, but now she has had it explicitly explained to her.

Both parties have now – as can be seen from Figure 5.2 – increased the amount of openness between them. The junior nurse began the process by revealing her reactions from her 'concealed self' and feeding these through to the staff nurse's 'blind self'; the staff nurse reacted non-defensively and revealed something from her 'concealed self', feeding this through to the junior nurse's 'blind self'.

The conversation might then go as follows. The junior nurse may say to the staff nurse:

'I accept your view that I might not be doing this as competently as possible, and I would welcome some help and instruction in how to do it. However, at the end of this I would like to feel that I was capable of doing it by myself. Would you be willing to help me?'

The staff nurse is almost bound to reply 'Yes'.

This is what psychologists call being more 'open' with each other. The process of interchange that has been described above builds trust between people because they are able to clarify each other's motives and discuss the impact of their communication and behaviour on each other.

If the staff nurse had reacted defensively to the initial response from the junior nurse she might have said to herself, 'Why should I bother? She is not worth it. Let the thing go wrong and I will have to sort it out anyway in the end, and that will show her just how incompetent she is'. In this circumstance, the patient may have suffered and, of course, the relationship between the two parties would have been diminished. Then, the next time the staff nurse would see the junior nurse doing something slightly incorrectly she would not comment on it and there would be no opportunity for the junior nurse to know how to do the job better or to generally improve her performance.

As you will have gathered, there are some skills in giving feedback to people that do not arouse their defensiveness. These will be touched on later when the problems of giving feedback are addressed. The purpose of mentioning this here has been to add to the discussion of the problems of communications with people who are difficult, or may become difficult, as, when there are relationship problems, communication problems can become even more acute. What is needed is an ability to build up a relationship of openness between the parties so that they can explore these differences.

The process of building such a relationship can be begun by one party genuinely listening to what the other party is saying, trying to understand what is going on in the other's mind and how they are feeling. The skill is that of listening. Being able to listen openly and non-judgementally to what the other person is saying is a key change tool. Strangely enough, the very fact of listening can actually change someone's behaviour. So successful is it that there is a school of counselling that is on this particular precept, and, of course, the Samaritans organization works so well because this is what the people on the phones do – listen to the other person in a non-judgemental and open way.

The next chapter moves on to cover another aspect of communications, namely that of building rapport with the other person. A major component of this is the skill of listening, and this is looked at in more detail in Chapter 6.

Chapter 6

The Rapport-building Tool

You may wonder why you need to build up rapport with your difficult people. It may, in fact, be the very last thing on your mind – and certainly the last thing that you want to do. Nevertheless if you can get on the same wavelength as they are, you can become more influential and have more chance of achieving the outcomes you desire. What, though, is rapport?

Having a rapport with someone means that you are able to understand how they see the world and can see things from their perspective. You are genuinely able to understand the problems and difficulties that they are experiencing. Likewise, you encourage them to understand how you see the world and issues that are important to you.

When you have a rapport with someone they are more likely to be persuaded by you because they see you as like themselves rather than different to them. It is easier to build up rapport with someone you like and who shares the same interests as you. It is harder where the other person is different to you and there is little positive feeling between you. Nevertheless, the rapport tool can be a powerful one for you to use in dealing with your difficult people. The reason for this is that the difficulties they experience are probably not only with you but with other people, too, and, therefore, they will appreciate a relationship that demonstrates an understanding of their problems. How do you do this?

Paraphrasing

One very powerful technique comes back to the discussion we were having about communication and listening. This is the technique of paraphrasing. It sounds very simple but it really is very powerful in terms of its rapport-building potential, which leads on to being able to change another person.

What is it?

Paraphrasing is 'playing back' to the other person what you thought they were saying to you, using your own words. So, if they are putting a point or argument to you, you will respond to that point not by commenting on it, but by saying back to them what you understand them to be saying. You are 'entering' their world, not confronting them with your world – this can come later.

The Lionel den

Take the case of Dr Sam Lionel, an irascible consultant surgeon. The business manager in his directorate, Jennie Digby, has been asked to get Dr Lionel's agreement to changing the starting time of his clinics, which currently begin at 9.30 am. For reasons that do not concern us here, the Out-patients Department Manager wants all clinics to start at 9 am. Jennifer approaches Dr Lionel and asks if she may have a discussion with him about out-patients clinics. He agrees to meet with her after his current clinic finishes and so they meet again at 4 o'clock in the afternoon.

Jennifer starts the discussion by saying something along the lines of, 'Dr Lionel, as you may know, the Out-patients Department Manager is hoping to arrange for all clinics to start at 9 am and I was wondering what your views on that are.' Dr Lionel replies by saying, 'I have been doing my clinics starting at 9.30 for the last 5 years and I have no intention of changing – it will really upset all my other arrangements.'

Jennifer paraphrases what he said back to him: 'Can I just check that what you are saying is that you find it unacceptable to begin at 9 am and that the consequence of starting at 9 am would be that other arrangements that you make could not be stuck to?'

Dr Lionel says, 'Yes, that is right. I do my ward round at 8.30 am each morning, which then gives me good time to begin my clinics at 9.30 am. There is no way that I could begin my clinic at 9 am because I would then not have time to do my ward round properly.'

Jennifer plays back to Dr Lionel what she heard him saying. 'So, the problem, Dr Lionel, is that if you were to start at 9 am, then this would not give you sufficient time to undertake the ward round as you would wish.'

Dr Lionel agrees that this is what he said. Jennifer then says, 'Would it be possible for the ward round to start half an hour earlier, at, say, 8 am?'

Dr Lionel replies, 'No, I couldn't do that because the day staff would not really have had time to get themselves organized on the ward and I insist that they have a full picture of all the patients and what has happened to them overnight before I begin the round.'

Jennifer then plays that back to Dr Lionel 'What you are saying is that it is important in doing your ward round that the day staff are fully conversant with all the problems staff might have had during the night.'

Dr Lionel then agrees that that is the correct statement of the case. Jennifer then continues, 'Supposing we were able to change the shifts of the nursing staff so that the day staff came on a little earlier, would that make life a little easier for you?'

Dr Lionel agrees that it might.

Jennifer then goes away to investigate the possibility of shifting the beginning of the day staff shift.

At all stages of the discussion, Jennifer tries to check that she has fully understood what Dr Lionel's reservations are. Once she knows what these are, she then feels able to suggest possible options for meeting his requirements as well as the Out-patients Department Manager's requirements of starting clinics at 9 am.

Because Dr Lionel has a reputation for being irascible, the discussion could otherwise easily have spilled over into an argument about administrators and doctors, bureaucracy and red tape. However, because Jennifer was able to show understanding, she avoided the 'red rag to the bull' syndrome.

Paraphrasing, as you can see, is very useful. The one thing to be careful about is that you do not paraphrase after every point made by the person you are having a conversation with. If they were to say to you, 'Good morning', and you responded by saying, 'What you are doing is bidding me the time of day', this would clearly be unacceptable and, indeed, ridiculous. However, when you genuinely want to show that you do understand the point made by the other person, paraphrasing is very effective. Not only does it do this, but it also starts to build up the relationship because you are showing that you are trying to understand the world as Dr Lionel (in this case) sees it, and sharing to some extent the world as you see it once you have built the relationship a little bit.

Paraphrasing can be very useful in a variety of circumstances, but is especially so when you have conflict and you are having to deal with difficult people. It helps you build up the relationship so that you can see things as they see things.

One word of advice, though. As you begin to understand their world, it is quite conceivable that you may want to change your own views to accommodate what you now see is the rationale of their views. This, of course, is perfectly acceptable, providing it meshes in with your outcomes or you can change the outcomes in such a way that the results will be acceptable to you.

There are one or two other, slightly more esoteric techniques that you can use for building up rapport with someone else. The first of these is called 'mirroring'.

Mirroring

If you see two people in a restaurant enjoying a meal together, you may notice that as one leans forward, so does the other; as one leans back, so does the other; as one begins their soup, so does the other and so on. The mirroring occurring here is quite unconscious, but you can use this technique quite consciously.

What the mirroring technique amounts to is the emulation of the body posture of the other person you are talking to. Obviously you have to be discreet about this. If they should suddenly scratch their head and you do exactly the same, then they will think that you are playing games with them. However, if your movements are too subtle, then they will not be noticed by the other, who is subconsciously observing that you are like them. As before, you are more likely to change someone's behaviour if they see you as being similar to them.

If you are skilled in mirroring, you can check your state of rapport by 'pacing' the other person. Here you take the lead in, say, sitting forward, and note whether or not the other follows your lead. If they do, then you have rapport. If they don't, try some paraphrasing or more mirroring.

It is obvious from the above that you have to use these tools with care and subtlety. If the other becomes conscious of what you are up to – especially with mirroring – they will see you as playing games with them, which inhibits your chances of changing the other quite considerably.

You can practise these skills in 'safer' environments – for example, with friends and family where the consequences of being detected will be less significant. Don't forget that these tools demand skill in their use, but that they can be acquired like any other skill, by practising.

So far, the focus has been on how you can build on the relationship so that you can discuss the problems between you more openly – in line with the discussion of Johari's window. However, at some stage, you are going to have to give the other person some feedback on how they are perceived. How you can do this effectively is the subject of the next chapter.

Chapter 7

The Feedback Tool

Revisiting Johari's window, you will recall that one quadrant was to do with the 'blind self'. This is behaviour of ours that others know about but we don't. People may be being difficult without realizing how their behaviour impacts others – they need for their 'blind window' to be opened. This is the process of giving feedback. However, you will recall from the earlier discussion on communication filters that a filter called 'defensiveness' was commented on. People try to protect themselves from comments that they see as threatening the image they have of themselves. They do this by denying the validity of others' views and reactions.

The feedback tool uses processes to try and avoid the defensive filter so that communication by you to the difficult person about their behaviour, at the minimum, actually 'registers', rather than being filtered away.

The extent to which you need to use the tool depends on your assessment of how defensive the other person is to comments that you want to make about their behaviour and attitude. Some people can take it 'straight from the shoulder' and are very open to comments from others, however negative they might be. On the other hand, there are people who, as discussed earlier, will reject any form of criticism, however valid. These are the highly defensive people. As a generalization, people who can be rather difficult in their relationships with others also tend to be rather defensive. In deciding whether or not to use this tool, you might find looking at Figure 7.1 quite interesting. This is a matrix that helps in analysing levels of defensiveness together with levels of job performance.

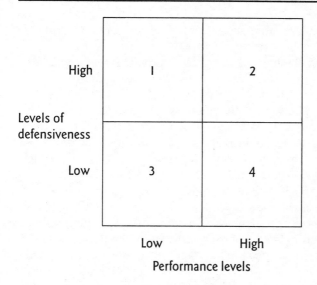

High   1   2

Levels of
defensiveness

Low   3   4

Low   High

Performance levels

Figure 7.1 Performance and defensiveness matrix

Performance and Defensiveness

If, for example, your difficult person performs the majority of their job well and gives a high level of performance, but is also highly defensive, they will fall into box 2 in Figure 7.1. There are significant feedback problems to such a person. This is because of the danger that the feedback might affect their performance very negatively. It is with these people that you particularly need to use the feedback tool described later in this chapter.

If, on the other hand, your individual fits into box 1 – they are highly defensive, with a low level of performance (this, incidentally, is often the case) – then, again, you need to tread carefully, but perhaps not be too concerned about the impact on their performance, which is of a low standard already. It may be that, with this particular type of individual, the confrontation tool that is discussed on page 59 could be particularly useful.

The easiest type of 'difficult person' to deal with is one who falls into box 4 – performance is high and defensiveness low. People of this type work well and are willing to accept criticisms without filtering these out. In this case, your communication can be much more direct and the language patterns may not need to be quite so. In effect, they are not really 'difficult'.

Those who fall into box 3 have both low defensiveness and very low performance. Often these people are just grateful for any comments that will enable them to improve their performance. However, it is also very likely that their level of motivation will be pretty low and you may have to work on this to lift up their performance once you have given them the feedback. These people have what is often referred to as a low self-efficacy, more of which later in discussion of the motivation tool (see page 71).

You may find this way of thinking about performance and defensiveness is especially useful when you are having to appraise the performance of a difficult subordinate. Often, such performance appraisals tend to have a negative impact on the performance of individuals because they are handled rather clumsily. If the feedback tool is not used with skill, you can reduce a high-performing individual to somebody who is a low-performing one with concomitant high levels of defensiveness.

After you have analysed their performance and defensiveness levels, you can decide how to use the feedback tool. In Figure 7.2, you will note the different behaviours arising from the various mixes of performance and defensiveness. The key to using the feedback tool is that it is non-evaluative, which is to say that you are not passing judgements on the difficult person. If you do make a judgement about someone else's behaviour, they can simply refute your views by arguing that that is only your perception and nobody else thinks like you do. When using the feedback tool, the language that you should use would describe the other person's behaviour in terms of your reactions to it, not your judgement about them.

So, for somebody who is overbearing in a meeting, you might say to them that when you are in a meeting with them you find it very difficult to 'get a word in edgeways' and this causes you considerable frustration. If you have a rough assessment of how much time they spend talking compared with others, you could also say that this is because '80 per cent of the time you are doing the talking and that leaves only 20 per cent of the time for the rest of us'.

This gives the clue to the second characteristic of the feedback tool: what you say should be specific rather than general. To say to someone that they 'rub people up the wrong way' because of the way that they deal with them is too general. However, if you were

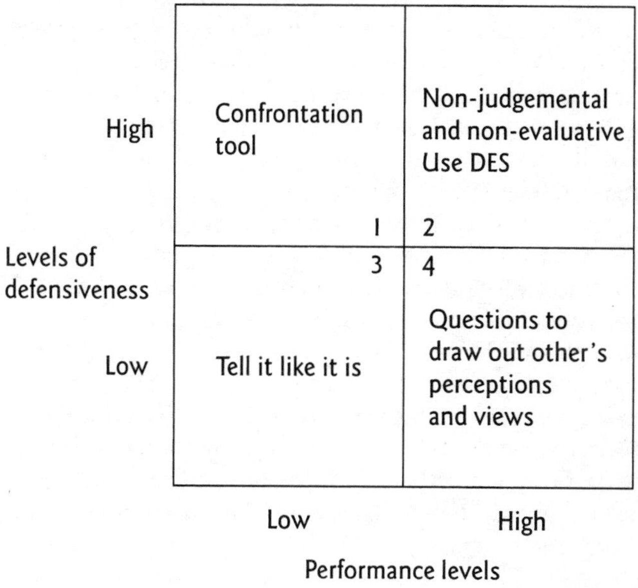

	Low	High
High	Confrontation tool 1	Non-judgemental and non-evaluative Use DES 2
Levels of defensiveness	3	4
Low	Tell it like it is	Questions to draw out other's perceptions and views

Low   High

Performance levels

Figure 7.2 Options for behaviours to adopt when giving feedback

to say, 'When we were having the discussion the other day about ward rotas, you made me very angry because you dismissed my ideas without giving me any reasons for doing so,' here, the feedback tool is being specific about behaviour that has caused the frustration rather than a vague statement of discontent. Sometimes we are tempted to give feedback to punish the other person because they have been so difficult. In some ways it makes us feel better that we have 'got it off our chest'. However, then the feedback tool is being used to satisfy your needs and not necessarily to change the behaviour of the other party. Remember all the time that you are trying to achieve specific outcomes, in terms of changes in behaviour, and that although you may feel better for unloading your angst, it does not necessarily do anything positive as regards the other person's behaviour.

Finally, remember to use the tool only on the type of behaviour the other person can do something about. If they have an irritating 'tick', there is very little they can do about this so there is not much point in drawing their attention to it.

Using the feedback tool is a skilled process and, however open an individual is and non-defensive, it is not easy to receive critical feedback. Often it is hard for someone to admit that they are not as good or as effective or as successful as they wish they were. Also, don't forget that most people have spent some time building up the image they have of themselves and in maintaining their sense of autonomy. What you are trying to do is change their behaviour in ways they may not have considered.

In summary, the feedback tool is built on the acronym DES, meaning *d*escribe the behaviour, *e*xpress your reactions and *s*pecify what you will do, but not as a threat. For example, George is always popping into your office for a gossip. You are getting behind in your own work, so you might say to George:

> 'George, you have visited my office four times already today. I'm getting frustrated and angry because I am now getting behind with my work. What I propose is that I see you at 5 o'clock each day and at any other time I will ask you to leave unless the matter is very urgent.'

You will know that you have used the feedback tool well when the other person comes back to you and asks for your views on how they have performed or related to another person in the future.

When you use the feedback tool, be prepared for a discussion about the feedback, but be careful about falling into the trap where the other person asks you 'What do you think I should do?' The danger here is that it is tempting to give advice and, as you give it, each bit of advice is knocked down as being inappropriate, unsuitable or unworkable. Much better is to ask the receiver of the feedback what they think they might do to change or improve things. In other words, turn the question back on them. You could do this relatively easily by using such phrases as, 'Well, I am not sure what you might do, what do you think?' and then, as they start talking, ask further questions so that eventually they end up with their own small action plan that leads to changes in their behaviour.

Chapter 8

The Confrontation Tool

It may be that the feedback tool still does not produce the requisite changes in the other person's behaviour – they remain difficult or unwilling to accept the new conditions under which they have to operate. Where this is the case, you may have to go for the jugular! 'What do you mean?', you may ask.

Well, from Chapter 7 on the feedback tool, you will recall that the aim of it is to avoid the likely reactions of defensiveness to the behaviour being criticized and enable the other persons to maintain their image of themselves. However, there are occasions when this will not work and the feedback has to be a great deal more direct, evaluative and aimed at changing the self-perceptions others have of themselves. This is what the confrontation tool does.

The essence of the confrontation tool is that you challenge the behaviour of the other person and accept no explanations for the legitimacy of that behaviour. You demand changes in that behaviour and may use threats to support those demands. In using this tool, what you must avoid is an argument. You are to be direct, immovable and demanding.

As with all the other tools, careful preparation is needed before you use the confrontation tool. In particular, you need to be sure of your own ground. If you take the steps set out below, and note how these are put into practice in the example of the tool in use that follows, you should effect the desired result.

- **Step 1** Prepare the evidence that you are going to present to the other person and ensure that you have support for any threats that you intend to use.

- **Step 2** Prepare, and possibly rehearse, precise points you are going to make and how you are going to make them, being absolutely clear about the action you wish the other person to take.
- **Step 3** In this step you are 'setting the stage'. The confrontation meeting should be formal and businesslike. You should arrange that there are no external interruptions when you are using the confrontation tool.
- **Step 4** Convene and conduct the confrontation meeting, in quite a formal way. Formality makes it easier to deal with a difficult person in this context. Demand agreement to the changes you want. Do not argue about or debate these.
- **Step 5** Implement the monitoring processes to check that the outcomes of the meeting are being implemented.
- **Step 6** If necessary, conduct a review after a period of time to see whether or not the change in behaviour has actually manifested itself.

Turning now to the content of the tool, let us flesh out these bare bones of the technique by means of an example. First, though, it is important to recognize that when you confront somebody with evidence that challenges the image they have of themselves, you are likely to create some shock or disturbance in them. You therefore need to give the person time to digest the points that you are making. It is quite likely that the confrontation tool will engender some silences between you and the other person; be prepared for these and live with these silences.

Now to the example, which will take you, step by step, through the use of the confrontation tool.

The ophthalmologist who could not 'see'

Frank is the Chief Executive of a Trust. The Trust is generally successful and enjoys good relations with the majority of GPs.

For some time now, Frank has been hearing complaints from GPs that the ophthalmologist Hugh Spier refuses to write discharge letters about his patients to the respective GPs. His argument is that

GPs are not competent to look after eyes and therefore they do not need discharge letters. The GPs, quite naturally, find this insulting and have now written to Frank complaining about Hugh's behaviour. Prior to this, Frank has had the odd quiet word with Hugh, asking him to change his policy, but Hugh has always slipped around this request and carried on as before. Frank has tried talking to him several times since, but to no avail. He is now very frustrated.

Frank has invited Hugh to a meeting. They sit down in Frank's office, Frank being formal and sitting behind his desk. Because they do know each other reasonably well, they use each other's first names, though Frank is presenting a fairly cold and distant persona to Hugh. Frank opens up the discussion by putting the points he wishes to make to Hugh. He says something along the following lines:

> 'Hugh, I have received a number of written complaints from GPs about your unwillingness to write discharge letters about their patients to them. They are angry about this and are threatening to take the ophthalmology work away from the Trust. This I do not want, and I am sure you do not want it either. I have spoken to you many times about this, but to no avail. I now insist that, for all the ophthalmology patients you see, you will write a discharge letter to the respective GP within a week of the patient's discharge.'

Hugh responds to this by denying the need and putting the old argument that the GPs are incapable of looking after his patients so why on earth should he write discharge letters that just take up administrative time when he is a very busy person anyway. He goes on to question who the GPs think they are and ends by refusing to write the discharge letters as requested.

Frank listens carefully to the points Hugh makes, but will not comment on these because, if he does, he will just get into a slanging match with Hugh. Frank puts the demand again to Hugh and again asks Hugh to change his behaviour. Hugh refuses to do this and blames the GPs for stirring up trouble, administration for interfering in medical matters and says that there is a shortage of resources, particularly secretarial resources, to do this anyway.

Frank listens to Hugh's further angry outbursts, but does not comment. There is likely to be some silence between Hugh's statements. Once Hugh has vented his anger, Frank again repeats the changes that he wants Hugh to make. At this stage, Hugh's most likely reaction is to challenge Frank and say to him, 'What if I refuse to change?'

Frank should ignore the challenge but respond to the 'What if. . .?' question by saying that unless he, Hugh, does change, then it is likely that action will be taken to terminate Hugh's employment with the Trust. It is important to note here that, prior to the meeting, Frank checked with his Medical Director and Chairman that they would support this particular line of action. They both agreed and it may be that, at this stage, Frank wants to make this point to Hugh as well. Hugh is likely to respond to this with silence while he thinks about the implications. It is important that Frank is also silent, to give Hugh maximum time to cogitate on the implications of what Frank has said.

Hopefully, by now the confrontation tool has done its stuff and Hugh will acknowledge that he will have to change, otherwise he will lose his job. He may well change, but with an attitude of bad faith or unwilling compliance. Whatever turns out to be the case, it is important for Frank to check that Hugh is going to change. He can do this by asking Hugh directly what he proposes to do and when he proposes to start doing it. If the response is not in line with the outcome that Frank wanted, then, again, Frank will have to repeat precisely what he wants Hugh to do until Hugh acknowledges this and agrees to it.

The meeting will probably end with Frank saying to Hugh that he will put this agreement in writing and will be monitoring his compliance with it for the next period of time. It may also be the case that, at this stage, Frank wants to reinforce the point that should Hugh backslide on the agreement, the consequences could be dire for his employment.

The letter setting out what Hugh has agreed to do should be sent to Hugh immediately after the meeting, obviously marked 'Personal and Confidential'.

In summary, the stages that Frank went through in the meeting were as follows.

- Frank put the point to Hugh, but expected denial.
- Frank listened, but did not comment on the denial and put the

point again, expecting further denials and the blaming of others including himself.

- Frank listened, but did not comment on these denials and remained silent – the reaction from Hugh was further outbursts.
- Frank did not react, he remained silent.
- Frank stated the changes he required in Hugh's behaviour and Hugh reacted, as expected, with challenge and 'What if. . .?' question.
- Frank ignored the challenge and responded to the 'What if. . .?' question with threats that he had already checked as being viable. The likely reaction, which occurred, was silence. Frank also remained silent until Hugh acknowledged that he would have to change, either because he felt cornered or he recognized that he was willing to comply for whatever other reason. Frank replied by stating what the agreement was, from that point onwards, and asked Hugh to acknowledge that this was a correct interpretation of what was going to be done. Frank expects Hugh to comply with what has been agreed, but is aware that he may not do it exactly as Frank wants and so the conditions of the agreement may need to be restated.
- Finally, Frank pointed out that he would be putting this in writing to Hugh and, if appropriate, would arrange another meeting to see how the changes were actually working out.

The confrontation tool brings about a catharsis and, once the air has been cleared on what might have been a long-festering problem, all parties seem to feel better as a result. It is not pleasant having to use threats in this way, but where a person is highly defensive it is often the only way to get them to change their behaviour.

The critical issue for the confronter is to ensure that they do not become involved in an argument about the facts or perceptions. If this happens, the tool degenerates into a slanging match – hence the importance of a rehearsal before the tool is actually used. By this is meant that the confronter prepares themselves in terms of what they are going to say and what they expect will be the likely response of the other party and how they will respond to that. In this way, careful planning will enable you to remain cool and calm during the course of the confrontation and avoid it developing into a full-scale argument.

In summary, the confrontation tool is obviously particularly useful when people are highly defensive and difficult. If they are low performers, then you may not be concerned about losing them from the organization anyway. However, if they are high performers with a difficult 'trait', then the tool needs to used with great care because the last thing you want to do is reduce a high performer to someone who is just passing the time of day in their job. It is important to maintain their motivation while they are changing their behaviour in other respects. You may be able to do this by recognizing and acknowledging their strengths while pointing out the behaviour that needs to change.

Chapter 9

The Temperament Tool

You will almost certainly have heard someone explain disagreements and conflicts between two people as personality clashes. Undoubtedly personalities do clash to the extent of making it almost impossible to work with someone with a different personality. The purpose of the temperament tool is to aid understanding of the potential causes of such personality clashes.

The rationale for the temperament tool is that an understanding of why people are different helps us work more positively with such people. Differences, in other words, can be valued although they are often seen as problems. Indeed, the temperament tool does not provide prescriptive solutions for handling difficult people. Rather, it provides a way of understanding the causes of those differences and, once these have been established, it is possible to work out a way of living with them.

One of the difficulties that arises when we try to understand people is that there are so many, varied factors that go to make up behaviour that any one approach is bound to be limited in its usefulness. Nevertheless, even a limited understanding does help us organize our observations and thoughts and leads us into new ways of handling difficult colleagues. I am sure you have come across such phrases as:

'He is not the right type of person for the job.'
'She cannot get herself organized.'
'He will not meet deadlines.'
'She is always considering sky-blue possibilities.'

These observations are manifestations of a particular temperament type, and it is temperaments that are the basis of this tool.

Jung, the psychoanalyst, developed a theory of personality. Isabel Myers, a psychologist, developed the theory, describing 16 temperament types, or 16 different kinds of people. The key concept of the approach is that of preferences, that is to say that people have a preferred way of behaving. For example, if you write with your right hand and find this the most comfortable way to write, being right-handed is your preference. It does not mean that you cannot write with your left hand – it is just that this would be less comfortable for you. Your preference is to be right-handed. It is the same with the temperament types. You have a preference to behave in certain ways and the characteristics of these preferences create what Myers called 'psychological types'.

The value of the theory is that it provides insight for individuals into the sorts of people they are and the sorts of jobs or activities they prefer and find most fulfilling. In dealing with difficult people, the value of temperament types is that they give a greater understanding of other people and the differences between them and ourselves because it offers a way of classifying observable behaviours.

The best way to develop this understanding is by using a questionnaire developed by Myers and her daughter, Briggs, referred to as the 'Myers-Briggs type indicator'. However, such a questionnaire is not always accessible to everyone and so what follow are descriptions of the various types that will enable you to ascertain, rather crudely perhaps, but usefully, what your own preferences are and what the preferences of other people might be.

David and Alan in conflict

Consider two people – David Fisk and Alan Cash – who have what is termed a 'personality clash'. They work together in the Personnel Department of a large Trust. Alan is a gregarious sort of person and loves to pop into other people's offices and have a chat, talking over business and other practical issues.

David tends to work on his own, finding that he can achieve more by sitting at his desk, working things out himself. He is intensely irritated by Alan popping in for his chats.

When they are in a meeting together, David tends to be the ideas person and, although not very comfortable at meetings, will put forward his ideas and possibilities. Alan tends to 'pooh pooh' these, explaining how they won't work and accusing David of being a 'blue-sky dreamer'. This upsets David a great deal, who then retires into his shell. Alan then tends to take over the meeting and talks about the practical things that have to be done to achieve the various objectives and meet the deadlines.

David sees Alan as being rather insensitive and, despite his working in the Personnel Department, thinks he has little feeling for people. Indeed, Alan is very analytical about what has to be achieved and comes across to David as rather a cold fish when dealing with the 'people aspects' of the business.

David on the other hand is very concerned about the ways in which people are motivated and the impact of policies and object-ives on their motivation and their commitment to the Trust. David often accuses Alan of being heartless and inconsiderate, explaining to Alan how his ideas won't work because they take no account of people. In turn, Alan, as you might imagine, accuses David of being 'soft' and arguments develop and rage between them.

Alan is highly organized and enjoys meeting deadlines and sets deadlines for his staff. David, on the other hand, is always looking for better ways of doing things and finds deadlines irksome because they sometimes prevent him exploring other possibilities that he has in mind. Alan accuses David of being disorganized and David counter-accuses Alan of being a hard-driving manager. In meetings, arguments flare up, with each accusing the other of being incomp-etent, lazy, disorganized, unfeeling and so on. Their different modes of working are, of course, reflected in their staff, who tend to work in two camps despite the necessity for a high level of cooperation between them. Yet, both men are good performers and get the job done.

Their boss, Tom Butler, has spoken to each of them and asked them to be more cooperative with each other. This works for a short time but then the rows flare up again. Fortunately, Tom has come across the temperament tool and is about to use this in an attempt to develop an understanding of both David and Alan and help them appreciate the differences between them and value them rather than use these points as an excuse for war.

The 'type' dimensions are:

- extroversion–introversion (E–I)
- intuition–sensation (N–S)
- thinking–feeling (T–F)
- judging–perceiving (J–P).

By completing the Myers-Briggs type indicator, an individual can see what combination of preferences they have. These are expressed as a combination of the relevant letters (ESTJ, INFP and so on).

The first dimension considers preferences in terms of extroversion and introversion. Those with a preference for extroversion find that their interactions with people are a real source of energy for them. They enjoy a multiplicity of relationships and probably have a strong network of people they know and can call on. The extrovert will have many friends.

On the other hand, those who have a preference for introversion tend to enjoy their own company and actually find being alone a source of energy. They find interactions with other people at meetings and parties draining and would prefer a small gathering where they can have intense discussions with just one or two people. Introverts tend to be rather territorial and guard their space. Unlike the extrovert, they will have a very small number of intimates.

It is important to stress, of course, that there is nothing right or wrong with either of these preferences – they are merely the way that people feel happier working or being. In the case of David and Alan above, you will readily see that David has a preference for introversion whereas Alan has a preference for extroversion. It is not unnatural, therefore, that they might rub each other up the wrong way, given this difference.

The next set of preferences that Myers and Briggs identify is for intuition or sensation. These names indicate the preferences an individual has regarding how information is gathered. Sensation types prefer information gathered in the form of observable evidence and by way of the senses, such as sight, touch, smell, feel and hearing. Intuitive types, on the other hand, like to gather information via their perceptions of the possibilities, relationships and meaning between various elements of information.

People with a preference for sensation tend to be very practical, organized people who like to deal with reality. They are good at observing details and tend to be accurate in the arguments they propose. Intuitive types, on the other hand, are interested in the possibilities of things. They tend to be innovative and enjoy speculating about hypotheses. They may well miss details but will enjoy metaphors and analogies that bring possibilities to life. They tend to be the visionaries and the dreamers whereas the sensation types tend to be the practical and organized ones.

Referring back to the case of David and Alan, you will see that David is an intuitive type, enjoying visions and possibilities, whereas Alan is a very practical, organized person, dealing with the evidence of hard data.

The next set of preferences is that for thinking or feeling. These relate to ways of making decisions and coming to a conclusion. It is important to stress that if someone is a feeling type, this does not mean that their decisions are totally based on emotions, whereas a thinking type of person will tend to be purely analytical. Rather, it means that a thinking type will tend towards making impersonal analyses of causes and effects, whereas a feeling type will tend to consider the personal consequences of decisions in terms of values and principles.

Individuals with a preference for thinking tend to use impersonal bases for making their choices. They are logical, rational and objective. As such, they can come across as being rather cold when deciding what to do. Those with a feeling preference have strong sets of values that will influence their choices. Their decisions tend to be more subjective, and they come across as being warmer people as they are considerate of others when coming to decisions. Again, in the case of David and Alan, you will see that David is a feeling type and Alan is a thinking type.

The final set of preferences relate to what Myers and Briggs call judging or perceiving. Those with a preference for judging tend to be most concerned about making the right decision and being sure that all the loose ends are tied up. They prefer being organized and having deadlines. On the other hand, those with a perceiving preference like to keep their options open and are always searching for more incoming information. They like to leave things open. Thus, David is a perceiving and Alan a judging type.

You may be saying at this point 'This is all very interesting, but how do I find out what someone's preferences are?' The answer to this is to observe their behaviour over time and see whether or not you can categorize it in terms of one of the eight preferences. It is important to stress that these are preferences and so you may find that someone is, for example, very socially skilled and so can employ behaviour that would not be their natural preference. They, thus, appear at ease in social gatherings although their preference might be for an intimate person-to-person chat. In the context of the purpose of this book, such nuances do not really matter. What we are concerned with is trying to understand what might be the causes of clashes of temperaments.

Over a period of time, you are quite likely to be able to identify the preferences someone has. However, even if you are not and you are having problems with the difficult person, it may be that you can discuss the various types with them and, together, identify where their own preferences lie. For example, a person who is very affected by change, but has a strong sensation preference, can find the change discomforting; they tend to prefer structure and stability. Somebody with a strong intuition preference, however, would find change stimulating and that this gives rise to further ideas for change and development.

Insight into one's own temperament generates self-understanding and, from this, a better ability to cope with events that might otherwise cause some upset. Discussing the various preferences with individuals will provide them with such insight into themselves and others. It will also provide you with some ideas about how you can manage relationships so that they become less difficult. For example, once Alan and David appreciated their differences, they were able to work more harmoniously with each other, recognizing what impact each could have on the other.

Should you wish to pursue this particular tool further, I can strongly recommend a book by David Kiersey and Marilyn Bates, called *Please Understand Me* (Prometheus & Nemesis UK, 1984).

In summary, the temperament tool is a way of organizing observations about people so that you can understand where potential differences might lie and explore how these can be used productively – rather than destructively – as in the case study of David Fisk and Alan Cash. Most people find the analysis interesting – particularly if they have been able to complete a Myers-Briggs type indicator questionnaire. You may find that someone in your Personnel Department is able to take you through such a questionnaire and it could be a valuable experience to do this.

Chapter 10

The Motivation Tool

The motivation tool encompasses a number of tools within the overall bounds of motivation. These include expectancy theory, the reinforcement tool and the context shift tool. For the purposes of the subject of this book, our definition of motivation will be 'drive that a person experiences to achieve some end'.

Expectancy Theory

Of the many cases discussed at my seminars on difficult colleagues, those featuring the problem of motivation occur most frequently. A typical case might be as follows.

The disappointed pharmacist

Sheila Radcliffe has just been appointed Chief Pharmacist to a small Trust. She came from another Trust where she had been Deputy Pharmacist and had been looking forward to taking on her new responsibilities. One of the candidates for her job had been Freda Lavell, a principal pharmacist at the Trust. Sheila had been at pains to consider how Freda Lavell might feel, having not got the job that she had applied for. Sheila tried to build Freda into her decision making and involve her in her plans for the development of the pharmacy.

Initially Freda had responded very positively to these overtures, but, after about six to eight months, it has been noticed that she is becoming less enthusiastic and starting to moan about her work and the fact that she seems to be carrying everybody else's responsibilities. These get progressively worse, with Freda doing the minimum necessary, just to get by, and criticizing all and sundry around her – particularly Sheila. She complains about the Trust's management, the inconsiderateness of doctors, her work colleagues, the sisters on the wards and so on. She starts to turn up late for work and uses any excuse to enable her to go home early.

Sheila is perplexed as to what to do and, after her analysis of outcomes and levers for change, she decides that the problem is a motivational one. The question for her is how can Freda's motivation for the job be enhanced?

Sheila decides to use expectancy theory to analyse the motivational problems she thinks Freda is experiencing.

What the expectancy theory model (see Figure 10.1) proposes is that a person's motivation is a function of a variety of factors. The first of these is the extent to which behaviour results in attractive outcomes or rewards for the individual. If that individual does not perceive that the results of their efforts will be of benefit to them, then they are unlikely to be motivated to perform. However, these perceptions are mediated by the expectancy that the effort spent will deliver a performance that leads to those outcomes. Effort requires an expenditure of energy and time and it may be that an individual might value the outcomes of their motivated behaviour, but the energy and time they have to devote to achieving these outcomes is too great a cost in terms of the benefit they would get from the rewards for that effort. Therefore, they will ask themselves 'What is the point of working hard?' when the rewards are, in their view, so little compared to the effort that they have to invest to achieve them.

The next consideration is the link between ability and effort and how these relate to meeting the requisite performance standards. In this case, an individual may say to themselves that they would be willing to invest time and energy to try and achieve the performance standards that are required to deliver the desired outcomes, but they do not have the abilities to achieve those standards. Therefore, again, such a person would see little point in driving

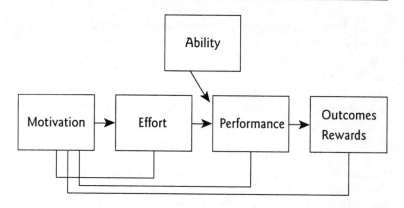

Figure 10.1 Expectancy theory

themselves to try and achieve the rewards, not because of a lack of energy and time, but because, in their view, they don't have the ability to deliver the performance that will achieve those rewards. Let us now return to Sheila and Freda to see how expectancy theory can be applied to an actual situation.

The disappointed pharmacist, part 2

Using expectancy theory, therefore, Sheila first of all begins by trying to identify those outcomes that Freda would experience as rewarding. In talking to some of Freda's colleagues, it becomes very clear to Sheila that one of the aspects of her work that Freda has enjoyed in the past is the research side of pharmacy. Prior to Sheila's arrival Freda had had free reign to undertake research – albeit on a small scale – into certain aspects of both pharmacy management and dispensing. She had published the results of her work in an international journal and, according to her colleagues, was over the moon when she saw her name in print.

Sheila now recognizes that Freda is strongly attracted to outcomes that enhance her professional reputation. This may or may not be concerned with her own career aspirations – she needs to check this out with Freda when discussing Freda's performance. Sheila then considers what Freda is having to do now. Essentially, she has to share the management of the pharmacy with Sheila. She has heard on the grapevine that Freda is complaining that this

73

doesn't give her enough time to do her research work and that she finds managing people particularly difficult. She much prefers to work on her own or with one or two others on a task the scope and objectives of which are clear. Sheila reckons that Freda does not see herself as being able to deliver a performance that will achieve outcomes that are attractive to her in terms of managing people, and that she probably also believes that she does not have the abilities to do this. These expectations have all impacted on her motivation to do her work.

Sheila decides to have a heart to heart with Freda, to try and work out with her what other outcomes might be attractive to her and how she could restore her motivation to work effectively in the pharmacy team.

In discussion, Freda confirms Sheila's analysis – although she says she has never thought of it quite as systematically as this. She confirms that, before, she enjoyed the research work and, in particular, the status that is attached to this – she especially liked her papers being published in association with a consultant physician.

Freda also confirms that she feels uncomfortable managing staff and seems to have to spend hours thinking about how to approach them to get them to do things in the way she wants them to. She says to Sheila that the game is just not worth the candle. She also explains that she has never been trained as a manager and is not really sure how to manage a team and delegate work to others. She does hope, however , that her considerable reputation as a pharmacist will enhance her career.

Sheila wants to retain Freda's obvious expertise in pharmacy and so decides to redesign her job so that it has a larger proportion of research in it. For example, Sheila has become increasingly concerned about the costs of some prescriptions and medicines. She asks Freda to investigate who is incurring these costs and what the outcomes of the treatment and prescriptions are. She confirms to Freda that she is happy for Freda to publish her results if she thinks this worth while. She also suggests to Freda that she might find it helpful to increase her managerial competencies and attend some training events. Freda is a little reluctant to begin with, but when Sheila points out that this will enhance her career possibilities, she agrees.

After these discussions Sheila and Freda agree that it would be sensible to review how things are working out in about two months' time, and to discuss then what Freda feels about the redesigned job and how it is going.

You will not be surprised to know that, as a result of her meeting with Sheila, Freda regained her motivation and became a high-performing member of the pharmaceutical team. Although she had never been really comfortable managing people, she certainly became better at this after some training. The Trust's management began to see Freda as a potential head of department.

Fortunately, the solution in this case was relatively straightforward. To summarize the way in which Sheila used expectancy theory, we can look at the three questions that ran through her mind.

'First, what value did Freda attach to the outcomes of her behaviour? Where these outcomes were of value, Freda was motivated; but where they were of little value, Freda was demotivated.

Second, to what extent did Freda reckon that she could invest the energy and time to deliver a requisite performance that would result in these valued outcomes?

Third, coupled with this last question, to what extent did Freda see that she had the competence or the ability to combine with the effort needed to deliver the requisite performance standards? Clearly, the way in which Sheila constructed the job for Freda after her appointment shows that Sheila's views were that she could not deliver the requisite performance requirements that would achieve her desired outcomes.

These three questions enabled Sheila to analyse the motivational problem behind Freda's behaviour.

Self-efficacy

Analysing Freda's difficulties has been fairly straightforward, so it hasn't been vital that things be gone into in detail, but now, to further understanding, it is necessary to examine one or two of the concepts in a little more depth – particularly that of ability.

As you will have noted from the discussion of expectancy theory, the basis of it is how a person perceives their own abilities. This process of perception of abilities is referred to as 'self-efficacy'. A person with strong self-efficacy – that is to say, someone who perceives that they have the abilities to undertake challenging work and tasks – will be persistent and overcome set-backs on the way to achieving the task. They will tend to be resilient people who can cope with failures and problems that occur as they are trying to achieve their objectives. They may well develop a variety of skills to enable them to cope better with the problems they are experiencing.

If, on the other hand, they have weak self-efficacy – that is to say, they perceive themselves as not having the abilities to undertake challenging tasks, then, quite naturally, they will tend to avoid these sorts of situations and challenges. They may also exaggerate their own personal deficiencies, saying such things as, 'Oh, I could never do that'.

An important aspect of self-efficacy is that it is set by a person's perceptions. If an individual has inaccurate perceptions of their self-efficacy on the positive side, they can become overconfident and so may become difficult people because they will undertake jobs that they are incapable of doing and immerse themselves into the mire. They may even tend to be rather boastful and irritate other people as well.

People who have weak and inaccurate perceptions of their own abilities on the negative side, tend to give up too easily and blame others for the difficulties they are experiencing. In Freda Lavell's case, Sheila believes Freda has weak self-efficacy when it comes to managing staff. She offers Freda some training in this and may then have built up Freda's perception of her abilities in this area by giving her tasks that involve working with small groups of people to start off with.

If, on the other hand, she had thought that Freda had an over-exaggerated sense of her own abilities, then she would have assigned tasks to Freda, requesting that Freda report on the plans she had for accomplishing those tasks. As the tasks had proceeded, Sheila would have asked for frequent and regular reviews of progress on the tasks.

An individual whose motivation is lacking can find themselves spiralling down into a situation where not only do they blame others for their uninteresting work, but also themselves for not having the abilities to undertake more challenging work. It is important to try and distinguish between motivation that creates the drive and the perception of ability or competence that enables the person to achieve the requisite performance.

You might find Figure 10.2 useful in this context. As you will see, on the vertical axis, competency levels can be described as being

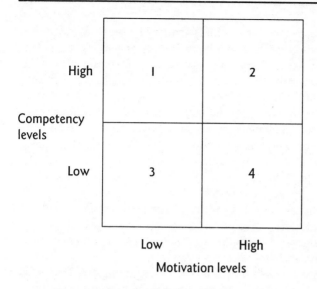

Figure 10.2 Motivation/competency matrix

either high or low. On the horizontal axis, motivation levels can be either low or high. Many difficult people tend to fall into box 3. Such people have low competency and low motivation. However, as explained earlier, it may be that the low motivation is a consequence of their perceived weak self-efficacy. In other words, they are not motivated because they don't think they have the necessary competencies to do well. In dealing with these difficult people, you need to assess where the problem lies. Is it because:

- the work offers few attractive outcomes to them
- they actually do not have the requisite competencies to achieve them
- they don't perceive themselves as having the requisite competencies to do this?

If the problem is of the first sort, your job is to find ways of making the outcomes more attractive. If the problem is of the second sort, then you need to train the individual. If it is of the third sort, you will have to show to the difficult person that, in fact, they do have the requisite competencies by, for example, having them undertake some small-scale assignments successfully, then building positively on these.

There are difficult people who fall into box 1 of the motivation/ competency matrix – they have high competency but low motivation levels. In other words, you know that they could do the job well, but their motivation, for whatever reason, is lacking. Again, you will want to check their perceived self-efficacy. In other words, do they see themselves as being competent or do they have weak self-efficacy and perceive themselves as being not so competent? If the latter is the case, then you will need to find ways of bolstering their confidence about their competency. This might be by giving them small projects to undertake to show that they can actually do quite challenging work. However, you do need to attend to the motivational aspects at the same time. In this you will be concerned about the outcomes that are attractive to the individual and whether or not they have the energy to combine with their competency to achieve the desired outcomes.

Box 4 is the mirror image of box 1. In this box are people who are highly motivated but are less than average in terms of competency. They are enthusiastic, but always seem to either mess things up or rush in where angels fear to tread. Again, you need to check whether this is because of weak perceived self-efficacy or they are actually incompetent. With these people, your main investment is in their training and development. The task is to build up their actual competencies and the individuals' realistic perceptions of these.

Take the case of Matthew – a major part of his job is to deal with patient complaints.

The quiet recruit

At the selection interview he had been quiet, but his ideas, when pressed, were good, and so Matthew got the job – on the basis that he would grow in confidence as he became accustomed to the new environment, and that this quiet appearance would calm the more difficult patients. Unfortunately, this has not been the case. If anything, Matthew appears awed by his superiors and is unwilling to participate in group discussions or to deal with dissatisfied patients, which his job requires him to do. While everyone had been happy to stand in for him at the outset and show him how best to tackle his work, the office is now too busy to show him what to do or to work around him.

Jacqui – who has ultimate responsibility for the staff – has talked to Matthew about his reluctance to participate. She felt that the discussion was productive, although she is unclear as to what to do next. Matthew said that other members of staff are far better at doing the job than he is as he has only just joined and, although he really wants to learn, he feels intimidated by their greater knowledge. During their discussion, Jacqui realizes that Matthew has, in fact, learnt a tremendous amount about dealing with patients and solving the problems the group is often faced with. It seems that confidence is the only thing Matthew lacks. In other words, he has a perception of his abilities that is too modest – he has a perceived weak self-efficacy.

Finally, in box 2 of the matrix are people who are highly competent and highly motivated. By definition, these people don't give you motivational problems – though they may give you a different set of problems, related, for example, to their interpersonal relationships.

Expectancy theory is a useful tool for helping you analyse motivational problems and, from this, propose solutions that would affect a person's behaviour. It is complicated because you are dealing with perceptions and expectancies, not necessarily actualities. Nevertheless, it is a powerful tool and should give you a framework for discussing motivational problems with your difficult people. To help you use it, see the checklist for the process of applying expectancy theory.

Checklist for the process for applying expectancy theory

It is best to tackle the application of expectancy theory in a series of steps, as follows.

Step 1: Identifying the motivation problem

Consider in what ways an individual's performance is not up to the standard you hope for or expect. Describe the behaviour of the individual or individuals and the situation in which the behaviour shows itself.

Step 2: Context of the problem

Identify the context in which the work is undertaken. This should help you analyse the problem. You should then be able to answer the following questions.

- What is the purpose of the work the individual undertakes and what do they have to do in terms of tasks to be performed?
- Consider in detail the individual whose behaviour you are hoping to change – for example, how old are they, what competencies and perceptions of these do they have, how long have they been in their job and so on?
- Is there anything else you should note down that might be valuable in analysing and understanding the problem?

Step 3: Present and future behaviour

Concentrate particularly on the behaviours that are actually observed and contrast them with those you want to occur (that is, the outcome). This step will be most valuable when you have completed it as specifically as possible.

Step 4: Analysis of causes

Write down what you see as being the major causes or factors that led to the performance problem. Remember that the causes of behaviour and performance problems can be classified as being to do with one or more of the following.

- **Ability** Perceptions of self-efficacy, sufficient information, expertise, capacity, skills, to do the job?
- **Desired performance** Is there a lack of understanding about what performance is actually required and expected?
- **Performance-to-outcome expectancies** How does the individual perceive the relationship between the outcomes and their performance?
- **Value of outcomes** To what extent does the individual value and/or appreciate the expected outcomes that would result from their performance?

- **Effort-to-performance expectancies** To what extent is the individual able to relate the connection between the expenditure of their effort and the achievement of their performance?
- **Individual needs** To what extent is the individual able to satisfy their own needs as a result of their efforts?

Step 5: Action planning

Now that you have identified the causes of the problem, the next stage is to change some aspects of the relationship between effort and outcomes. You might find the following questions helpful in this.

- What particular outcomes does the individual value? You will be able to assess these from observations and discussions. Try to list them in some order of importance. If you have insufficient information on them, what can you do to discover the things they do value?
- Are you clear about, and can you define, what expected performances you require and list these?
- Can you devise links between the outcomes and the performance? Here you are trying to find ways in which good performance can be reinforced. Make a list of them.
- Does the individual have the capacity to achieve these performance levels? In other words, are the levels that you require attainable by the individual? If you think they are not, what changes have to be made in the performance levels or in training the individual?
- Can perceptions of self-efficacy be more realistic?
- In what way can you monitor any changes in motivation and maintain constant surveillance over the relationship between effort, performance and outcomes?

You may like to apply the expectancy theory tool to the following case of Judith and Simon, who are medical laboratory assistants in a Trust in the London area.

Motivation in the path lab

Many staff on the point of retirement took advantage of early retirement packages when the first changes as a result of cuts in budgets and staffing came through, allowing staff numbers to diminish without too many forced redundancies.

Those remaining in the department find themselves doing increasingly diverse jobs, sometimes splitting their time between two projects that might previously have been the responsibility of two different departments.

Judith and Simon have never sought extra responsibility, but are competent, able employees who enjoyed the work they used to do and, likewise, enjoyed the social structure of the department. They have adapted to the changes. Although they now feel that they have to work much harder for the same money, they are good at what they do and their longevity of service makes them key members of the organization. However, after six months of hard work and stress, they are beginning to wish that nothing had changed, especially as their pay and working conditions don't seem to have improved and neither has the performance of the organization overall, from the statistics they see.

The more they discuss 'how it used to be', the less willing they are to be as flexible as their new jobs require and the more they feel exploited by their managers. Although their conversations started during tea and lunch breaks out of the lab, they are now spilling over into working time. The lab is open plan, too, which means everyone hears their dissatisfaction. As the weeks go by, their growing disillusionment and bitterness involve other members of staff, who, even if they have recently arrived, start questioning the amount of work they are being given and the rewards they are getting in exchange for doing it. Immediately after the change, productivity and morale were quite high, but now they are slipping as Judith and Simon relate how things used to be, and fuel employees' irritation at their managers' inability to notice their predicament.

Where would you say the motivation problem lies?

Reinforcement Theory

To reiterate something said at the very beginning of the book, everyone's behaviour is rational to them. The problem at the root of dealing with difficult people is that of working out what this rationale is. Reinforcement theory points out that people behave in a certain way because they get some pay-off or reward from that behaviour. Taking it one step further, what stimulates the difficult behaviour can be teased out and then it can be determined what the pay-off is from this behaviour. Take the cases of Jean and Bill, for example.

Jean and the GPs

Jean is a receptionist in a GP's surgery. Generally, Jean is fairly good at dealing with people and, although a little tense, is able to keep things well organized and under control. On occasions when the surgery becomes very busy and the telephones are ringing, however, Jean's behaviour changes. She starts to snap at the patients and deals with them as though they were children. Many patients have complained about this behaviour to the GPs.

In analysing Jean's behaviour, one of the GPs identifies the stimulus for it as being an increase in pressure when the normal tenor of the surgery is heightened because of more demands by the patients. This causes Jean to panic a little and she starts then to be rude to patients.

The pay-off for her of this behaviour is that the patients then tend to have little more to do with her as they don't want to have their heads bitten off again.

In this case, the discussion the GP has with Jean focuses on how she could better cope with the forces that cause her rather tart behaviour; how, in other words, the pressure can be reduced when it appears to be increasing.

Bill's pay-off

Bill, a junior administrator in a hospital, is well known for his difficult behaviour. He objects to taking on any extra work and is quick to complain to the Union should work other than that given in his job description be, as he puts it, 'loaded on to him'.

The pay-off for this behaviour is that nobody ever asks Bill to do anything extra or help out in any way. Bill has a quiet life. This is the pay-off he is getting and wants from his behaviour.

To change this behaviour, it is necessary to change the pay-off and, although Bill is set to go to the Union, his manager does not shirk from asking Bill to do extra duties when necessary and help out the others. The manager also makes sure that Bill (and others) are rewarded for their extra efforts by having time off in lieu. Eventually, Bill sees that his disagreeable behaviour is not leading to the pay-off that he initially desired and, after some time, the behaviour starts to change and he becomes a more willing member of the team. He particularly values the time off in lieu as it means he can, on occasion, have a whole day off in a week.

The model for reinforcement theory is much simpler than was the case for expectancy theory, but, nevertheless, it can create some insight into the causes of difficult behaviour. The sorts of questions that you need to ask to find out what stimulates the behaviour are set out in the stimulus and pay-off of difficult behaviour worksheet, below.

Stimulus and pay-off of difficult behaviour worksheet

1. Is there a specific situation that gives rise to the difficult behaviour?

2. Are there specific people who give rise to the difficult behaviour?

3. Is there a pattern to the difficult behaviour?

4. What has changed that might have an impact on the behaviour?

5. Turning to a consideration of the pay-off from the behaviour, you might ask the following questions.

   • What does the individual gain from this behaviour?

   • What advantages might the individual perceive that they get from the behaviour?

   • How do others react to the behaviour?

   • What changes as a result of the behaviour?

   • What other pay-offs might the individual appreciate?

Once you have answers to the questions in the worksheet, you may then have leads as to how you might change the behaviour by altering the nature of the stimulus or the benefit the pay-off gives to the individual. The 'stimulus-behaviour-pay-off' model is obviously very simple, but don't neglect it because of this – it can help you understand why people behave in certain ways and the pay-off that they get from this behaviour.

The temptation is to accept that a person is difficult and therefore do nothing about it – in other words, you enable them to enjoy the pay-offs from that behaviour. This, of course, just reinforces the difficult behaviour because they see that, by behaving in a particular fashion, the pay-offs that they value are the ones they get. This may make for a quiet life for you and them but can cause feelings of unfairness among other employees who may be willing to undertake, for example, extra work, even though they see the need for doing this. They look at Bill and his ilk, who are able to carry on in their own sweet way, and feel aggrieved that nobody tackles their uncooperative behaviour. Bill and his kind, on the other hand, are watching the others and amusing themselves with the fact that they have to take on extra work while they are able to get away scot free! The others are mugs, they are thinking.

Finally, let us move on to another aspect of motivation – the context shift.

The Context Shift Tool

The context shift motivation tool involves thinking about the degree of security a person experiences in their job. If your difficult person feels very secure in their job, then there may be little motivation for them to change unless future outcomes are perceived as being very attractive. Consultants who enjoyed a job for life had little motivation to change the way they behaved: they felt very secure. Now that job security is not so great, consultants, when confronted with the fact that their employment can be terminated more easily these days, realize that their levels of security are not as great as they were, creating more motivation to change.

The example given in Chapter 8 on the confrontation tool also shows the context shift tool at work. The ophthalmologist refused to send discharge letters to GPs, arguing that they were not sufficiently experienced to deal with eyes. Eventually the Chief Executive decided to use the context shift tool and the confrontation tool. His objective in doing this was to make the ophthalmologist aware of the fact that the security of his employment was not as high as he thought it was. In other words, he, the Chief Executive, would be willing to dismiss the ophthalmologist unless he changed his behaviour. When confronted with this realization, the ophthalmologist decided to change. In other words, if a person is feeling very secure, they are unwilling to change. Interestingly, if they feel very insecure they may also be unwilling to change.

Thus, the argument runs as follows. The only perceived security a person has is in what they are doing now, and, if they were to change, they fear exposing themselves to potentials that they do not fully understand. They will therefore stick to something they know.

In these circumstances, when an individual is confronted with the need to change, they become a stick-in-the-mud. Daphne is an example of this phenomenon.

The bossy ward clerk

Daphne is a ward clerk who is very bossy with both staff and with patients. Patients tend not to complain to her because they rather fear her bossiness. Nevertheless, they do mention their worries to the Ward Manager, Jill.

Jill decides to discuss the problems with Daphne. She points out to her that patients are complaining about her behaviour. Daphne argues that they never complain to her about this and what is happening is that the staff are conspiring against her to do her out of a job. She argues that since she came to the ward, everything has been much better organized because she makes sure things are filed away properly, the information systems are kept up to date and so on. The staff, she says, resent this because it requires them to be more systematic in keeping records and entering information on the computer.

Jill continues to pursue the point that Daphne is upsetting the patients with her bossy attitude, giving examples from her own experience and asking for Daphne's reactions to these. Daphne equally vigorously denies these and is quite convinced that everyone is conspiring against her. She rejects the evidence that Jill is offering to her and continues to behave in the same way.

Jill decides on a different tack. She finds out that Daphne is a single parent and very worried about losing her job because it took her a long time to obtain this one, which she enjoys. If she lost it, this would also mean extreme financial problems for her.

Jill approaches Daphne and opens the discussion by confirming to Daphne that she is doing a good job and that, in fact, the staff are appreciative of the way she has managed to get things organized. There is no doubt, Jill says, that the ward is being run better now than before Daphne arrived. She talks to Daphne about possible advancements and confirms to Daphne that she, Jill, is more than happy with the way she is administering the ward. Jill is trying to build up Daphne's feelings of security.

Once she is confident that Daphne does not feel so threatened, she then raises the question of Daphne's relationships with patients again. Jill acknowledges that Daphne herself has had no complaints from patients, but she confirms that she has. She hopes that Daphne can change because she is sure that, should Daphne be able to change her behaviour and her relationships with staff and patients, this will help her in her career in the hospital. She suggests one or two things that she might try differently. By increasing Daphne's feelings of security, Jill enables Daphne to listen more carefully to what is being said without reacting defensively or filtering out the views as being the product of a conspiracy by the ward staff. She appreciates that her job is not actually at risk so she doesn't have to defend her position and can therefore be more open to Jill's constructive criticism.

In summary, when you are trying to encourage a difficult person to change their behaviour, you do need to think about the context in which they are behaving as well as their motivations. You may, therefore, need to change their perceptions about the context of their employment security as people will change if they feel reasonably secure. If they feel very secure, however, they are unlikely to change and, equally, if they are very insecure they are less likely to change. In dealing with these people, you need to try to change their perceptions so that they feel reasonably secure in their work and can listen carefully to your views.

This chapter has dealt with a very complicated set of issues in dealing with difficult people. Motivation is not always easy to define or determine. You really need to understand the other party very well to fully fathom what their motivational drives are. What are the outcomes that they are seeking to achieve? Do they perceive themselves as having the necessary abilities to achieve these? Have they the energy and time to invest in delivering performance standards that would deliver the outcomes to them? How do they perceive their efficacy? Do they feel secure or insecure?

All these and other questions need to be answered before you can decide what changes to make to the job or to the context of the job to change the difficult person's behaviour.

Chapter 11

The Negotiation Tool

One way of gaining the commitment of a difficult person to the outcomes that you want is to negotiate a deal with them. This may feel like giving in to pressure, but it is not. Rather, it is a very sensible way of reconciling conflicting interests and needs.

Negotiation is sometimes seen as rather a dirty word. It is thought to be game-playing, with bluffs, counter-bluffs and devious tricks being used. Indeed, such negotiation might work well in the short run, but, when dealing with difficult people who will remain within the organization, it certainly will not work in the long term. It will, in fact, be counter-productive, so that those who play games and use tricks will rarely be trusted again and will have increasing difficulty in achieving any of their outcomes.

True, productive negotiation is about striking a deal that meets the interests and needs of both parties. When discussing the motivational tool, needs were discussed, looking at these solely from a psychological perspective. In negotiation, psychological needs are obviously important, but so are the material and resource needs anyone might yearn for. Indeed, it is these issues that negotiations tend to focus on. For example, take the case of Margaret Senior.

Pressure in X-ray

Margaret is a superintendent radiographer and has argued vociferously for extra clerical support in the Radiography Department. Margaret is a little prickly and very jealous of her own territory. She believes that others are conspiring against her – particularly the radiologists and managers – to take away her responsibilities. Unfortunately, Margaret does not run a very efficient department, but nobody has been brave enough to point this out to her.

Eventually, matters come to a head when the purchasers are complaining about the high costs of radiographic services and GP fundholders are threatening to take their business elsewhere. As far as Margaret can see, this is good news because then her department would be under less intense pressure and could probably manage with the existing clerical staff – providing the work did not increase and actually decreased.

This, however, is not the view of the directorate's Manager – Don Field.

Don knows how important income from GP fundholders is to the directorate and sees it as his mission to increase this revenue by increasing productivity and workloads. He is wondering how to tackle Margaret about this.

First, he identifies what Margaret's needs are. These, as he understands them, are to remain in charge of her department and have some additional support to enable her to cope better with the administration of the Department.

Don then spells out what his own desired outcomes are. First, to achieve Margaret's commitment to increased throughput in the Department, thereby generating a higher revenue stream, particularly from GP fundholders. Specifically, he wants Margaret to open the Department from 7 am in the morning to 7 pm in the evening, and he wants Margaret's cooperation in this.

Don decides to prepare the ground by raising the matter at his meeting with the heads of departments his department works with. These include physiotherapy, occupational therapy, radiography and pathology. The matter is raised in general terms in relation to the need to increase the throughput of GP fundholders' work to maintain the revenue stream. Don explains what will happen should such revenue streams not increase and points out that some departments may well be threatened because another Trust is interested in taking on this work. Don produces some figures to show the changes in workload that have occurred in the last 12 months and demonstrates what will happen if the trend continues. He ends the meeting on an optimistic note, arguing that there is no reason to assume that the future will not be bright for all the departments under his aegis.

Having prepared the ground in these general terms, Don then sets up individual meetings with the respective departmental heads, including Margaret Senior.

In his meeting with Margaret, Don explains what he hopes to achieve and watches her reactions, which are ones of dismay, if not downright frustration and anger. He lets Margaret vent her feelings on these and then seeks her cooperation to see whether or not there are alternative ways of achieving his outcomes. Margaret cannot think of any. Don then, very gingerly, raises the question of the management of the Radiography Department and invites Margaret to raise her concerns about the radiologists wanting to take the Department over, as well as the shortage of administrative staff.

Don then moves the negotiations on to the next stage by making an offer to Margaret along the following lines.

'Margaret, if you agree to try, for a pilot period, opening the Department for the hours that I am proposing, and also to examine the way in which work is scheduled through the Department, then I will guarantee, as far as I can, that you will remain in charge of the Department, and not be threatened in this by the radiologists. More than this, if you agree to these proposals, I will set in train a process for examining the administrative workload and, if that analysis confirms your suspicions that you do not have sufficient administrative resources, then I will provide whatever the analysis suggests is needed.'

Margaret questions Don hard on what guarantees he can actually give her and whether or not he can really give her additional administrative support if it proves necessary. Don sticks to his guns and asks Margaret to consider the deal. Margaret knows in her heart of hearts that Don has a number of options open to him if she does not agree to this proposal. Don, in his preparation for this negotiation, has considered what his best alternative to a negotiated agreement (BATNA) will be. Don has come to the conclusion that, should Margaret not agree, then he will ask the Clinical Director to impose the deal on Margaret. Should Margaret not accept this, then, inevitably, she will no longer remain superintendent and control of the Radiography Department will pass to the radiologists. Don, however, is very careful not to mention this, preferring to come to a negotiated deal with Margaret so that she is committed to trying out the new arrangements and can save face by pointing out that she is going to get extra administrative support if it proves to be needed.

After a few days, Margaret knocks on Don's office door and tells him that she is happy to accept the deal and asks if they can talk about the analytical process that will be necessary to identify any changes that may be needed in administrative support. Don readily agrees and together they sort out the logistics of opening the Department for longer hours, working out the best way to see patients through the Department to minimize costs and increase revenue. They agree they will try this out for a period of six months, after which time they will come together and review how the experience is going.

Don is pleased with the results, as is Margaret. Both have satisfied at least some of their needs in agreeing to the deal.

Examining this example in some detail, it is possible to see the stages that Don went through in considering how to negotiate with Margaret.

The Phases of the Negotiation Tool

First, Don was clear about the outcomes that he wanted, but he was also at great pains to identify the needs and interests that Margaret might have as well.

Second, he prepared the ground by raising the matter generally at a meeting of the heads of department so that the proposals he put to Margaret were not new to her and thus had a greater chance of flourishing than if he had suddenly confronted her with a new set of proposals and immediately afterwards tried negotiating with her. He also created a package of ideas for Margaret to consider, and was clear about his BATNA. In other words, he knew what he would do should Margaret not agree to his proposals. Having a BATNA gave Don strength in the negotiations because he knew that there were other options open to him.

Third, he was prepared to move himself and used phraseology such as 'Margaret, if you do this, then I will do that'. He was careful to ensure that what he was offering to Margaret met her needs and that the demands he was making of her would satisfy his needs.

Fourth, he gave Margaret time to consider before coming to an agreement.

Once agreement had been obtained, Don sent a note to Margaret confirming the deal, then went on to plan with her how it could be executed.

Finally, Don agreed with Margaret to review the negotiated deal six months hence to make sure that both were content with it and to see whether or not it needed modifying in the light of experience.

Using the negotiating tool enabled Don to deal with quite a difficult person who is very jealous of her own department. Yet, by identifying her needs, he was able to put together a package of proposals that was acceptable to both of them.

As with the use of all the other tools, negotiation involves preparation beforehand. You must understand the needs and interests of the other party and be absolutely clear about the outcomes you are searching for. You have to construct a package that meets their needs and your needs and also be willing to move and vary that package if necessary. In the negotiations in our example, Don did not need to make many changes to his package, but if Margaret had not accepted the extended opening hours, Don was prepared to modify this. For example, if Margaret had insisted on administrative support from the outset, then Don was willing to concede this, providing that it could be reviewed after the six months.

Once Don had got the deal with Margaret, they went on to implement the plan quickly after Don had made sure that the agreement was written down. He probably would not have asked Margaret to sign any documents, but there was an exchange of memos between them to ensure that they both fully understood what they had committed themselves to, and this is important.

The negotiating tool is also a very appropriate tool to use when you are dealing with difficult people who are your peers within your organization. You do not have any real power over them, but what you do have are resources that you might be able to put at their disposal, providing they agree to something that you require.

It is probably not the best tool to use with people who perceive themselves to be much higher up the organization than you. In such cases, they may see it as impertinent of you to think that you could do a deal with them. On the other hand, if they perceive that you have the backing of another senior member, such as the chief executive, then you will be able to negotiate deals quite straightforwardly, just as Don did with Margaret.

Chapter 12

The Role Analysis Tool

Shakespeare in *As You Like It* summed up the concept of roles. 'All the world's a stage, and all the men and women merely players: they have their exits and their entrances; and one man in his time plays many parts'.

Those many parts are the roles that people play during their lives. These include such parts as parent, child, breadwinner, churchgoer, doctor, nurse and so on. Role analysis takes as its starting point the fact that individuals do fulfil many such parts or roles in their lives. These roles are sometimes determined by those they work with, sometimes by their own innate desires and wishes, sometimes by circumstances.

Role Expectations

We all have expectations of how a person should behave and perform in a role. We would be disturbed if a doctor came to work dressed in grubby overalls with long, tangled hair. This is because such a mode of presentation does not conform to our expectations of what a doctor should look like. However, expectations can be more subtle than that.

What follows, therefore, are various ways of defining roles with examples of the possible 'difficult people' problems that can be created by role-related behaviour.

Role conflict

In an organizational setting, there can be conflict between roles or between what people expect of roles or how they fulfil them or how they perform them. In this chapter, some of these conflicts will be identified because they can give rise to people behaving in a difficult fashion. By being able to determine whether or not the cause of the behaviour is an aspect of the role or something else enables you to decide how you might tackle the problem. For example, Jill is experiencing role conflict.

Jill's problem

Jill is very hardworking during her office hours, although a bit introspective. Sometimes, though, she is required to work beyond the office hours because a clinic is running late. She refuses to do this and has got the reputation of being uncooperative.

Because Jill is so introspective, she has never explained to her colleagues that she has an elderly parent she has to look after and that if she stays late, the parent becomes very upset and angry with her. Jill is so keen to keep her job that she is reluctant to share her personal problems.

What we have here is a role conflict. Jill has one role as a hard-working receptionist in an Out-patients department and another role, which she considers to be just as important, as a carer to an elderly parent. Jill sometimes experiences extreme conflict between these roles, which creates stress and anxiety in her. When she is asked to do extra work she therefore becomes rather abrupt and is unwilling to explain why she cannot. People put this down to being uncooperative, but, in fact, it is nothing of the sort.

In an organizational setting, role conflict can also occur when an individual is accountable to more than one person. This is not to say that such a situation is undesirable, but you do need to be aware that it can cause difficulties for the person concerned and result in difficult behaviour, as it did in Bernard's case.

Bernard's story

Bernard is a personnel officer directly accountable both to a clinical director and to the Chief of Personnel in the Trust. Because there are conflicts over policy objectives between these two people, Bernard often finds himself caught as the proverbial nut in the nutcracker.

His easiest options then are either to side with one party, in which case he becomes known as a difficult person by the other party, or steer his own middle course, in which case he becomes known as a difficult person by both parties.

It is essential that role conflict of any kind be surfaced and discussed and a way of working determined that reduces the potential aggravation such conflict can cause. There should also be an opportunity for the 'actors' to come together to sort out conflicts and problems.

The unpopular successor

June's story

June has just been appointed Director of Nursing for St Olav's Trust. She follows a very popular nurse who is also a very successful general manager. June's colleagues expect her to be like her predecessor. For example, her predecessor used to do ward rounds regularly, knew all the nursing staff by name and was generally very sociable. June, however, prefers to work in her own office, seeing only a few people and tending to plan the development of the service on her own with one or two trusted colleagues.

By behaving in this way, June is not conforming to the leadership role that her colleagues expect of her. She comes to be viewed as someone who is difficult to know and with whom you would probably not discuss problems. Gossip soon starts and stories about June's lack of sociability gather momentum.

In some senses this may not matter, but in other ways it does because it can put pressure on June that might eventually lead to her departure. This would be very disappointing, because what is needed in this particular Trust is a strategic view of nursing for the future, which is what June is providing.

June's 'problems' can be analysed in terms of role expectations. June and the others need to discuss their different expectations of the Director of Nursing role and perhaps come to an agreement on how June might manage the role to better meet the expectations of the others while still maintaining her good strategic work. Alternatively, June might make it known that whereas her predecessor was a very successful pragmatic nurse, what is required now for nursing is someone who will take on a strategic role. In fulfilling this role, June has to behave differently to her predecessor, but this does not mean that she is any less committed to nursing and the nursing staff than her predecessor.

Role ambiguity

In organizations subject to change, it is not possible, nor even desirable, to define roles with absolute precision. This, however, does leave the scope of the role open for the individual to decide on or discuss with colleagues. Many functions, such as personnel or management services, have roles that are ambiguous in that role holders do not know what is expected of them, nor how their work will be evaluated. This can be both frustrating and demotivating, leading to work performance that is below standard and difficult behaviour.

The answer is to try and scope any one role so that there are clear areas of certainty and agreement. Where there are areas of uncertainty, these should be thrashed out so that the role holder is clear about what is and is not required in that role and how their performance will be evaluated.

Someone who suffers from role ambiguity is Angela Duckworth.

Angela's story

Angela is a clinical instructor and visits the wards to provide further clinical teaching and guidance to the nursing staff.

She believes that part of her role is to correct those nurses who are not following the procedures properly, which include administrative as well as clinical procedures.

Others do not think she has any 'jurisdiction' in some of these areas and accuse her of 'pushing her nose in where it is not wanted'. She is met with hostility and uncooperative behaviour, which makes her even more determined to do the job as she sees fit.

Life becomes so difficult that the Chief Nurse feels it necessary to call a meeting where the scope and boundaries of the clinical instructor role are carefully laid out and then agreed. This has the added benefit that it provides a clearer basis on which Angela's work can be assessed by the Chief Nurse.

Role overload

Role overload occurs when there are just too many demands being placed on a particular role. This can happen to some clinicians who take on the responsibilities of being a clinical director in addition to those of 'clinician'. They may also be active on local medical committees and interested in such things as clinical audit.

Dr Stephen Smith is one such character and Keith Hutton provides another example.

Stephen and Keith burn candles at both ends

Dr Stephen Smith is an excellent physician and, as such, was asked by his colleagues to become Clinical Director of the medical directorate in which he works. He has always been interested in management, as well as in the politics of medicine. He has thus also been involved in a number of the British Medical Association's working parties, as well as sitting on the Trust's medical committees.

In undertaking all these roles, he has begun to feel under pressure as there are many competing demands on his energy and time. Because he is swamped, he has become stressed and so argues with anybody who upsets his schedules, which are very tightly organized.

As the Trust is going through a financial crisis, this puts additional pressure on him to attend management meetings, which have started to take priority over his clinics. This has led to GPs complaining about the poor service they are receiving and a number of his diabetic patients complaining about the times when their clinics have been cancelled at short notice.

Under all this stress, he is irritable and very difficult to deal with. It is only when a colleague sits down with him and discusses all his commitments that he realizes just how he has overstretched himself by committing to so many different responsibilities and roles. He starts to solve his problems by prioritizing those areas that he wants to concentrate on and withdrawing from those he does not wish to pursue any further.

Keith Hutton provides another example of role overload. Keith is responsible for the IT systems in the Trust. In this capacity, he has to satisfy the demands of many 'customers'. His difficulties in doing this are exacerbated by the poor quality of the computer programs and the age of the equipment he has to work with. He often has to work late because there has been a breakdown during the day. Keith is experiencing some considerable pressures.

His colleagues find that it is impossible to say how Keith will behave when he comes in to work in the morning. Sometimes he is the very soul of jollity, makes tea for his colleagues, takes calls for them when they are busy and generally helps office life run smoothly. On other days, he appears to be the opposite, snapping in response to trivial questions and being curt to all concerned.

Keith works with a team and the deadlines for their projects can be tight, which means that everyone has to pull together, but, somehow, despite his volatile and occasionally uncooperative behaviour, the group has never yet missed a deadline. The stress levels, however, have been known to rise when Keith, whose role is primarily managerial, refuses to help the rest of the group run a program on the basis that 'they should have taken the time to learn it before the need arose'.

The partners of members of the group have suffered long evenings of complaints about Keith on his bad days, only to have to listen to those same people talk at equal length about how guilty they feel about how nasty they have been when Keith has a 'good day'. Keith is a familiar name to the families of everyone in the group, but not a welcome one.

Recently, Keith has been going through a particularly bad patch, to the point where Joanna, one of his key members of staff, loses her temper and a vigorous argument ensues, ending with Joanna in tears and Keith storming out. The next day, Keith brings in a bunch of flowers for Joanna, to apologize for upsetting her. Two weeks later, however, his new-found bonhomie has disappeared, and the same tense atmosphere has returned.

Keith is a classic case of role overload, probably with a pinch of role conflict in there as well.

You may like to think how you would handle this problem if you were a friend of Keith or his 'boss'.

Role underload

Role underload, naturally enough, is the opposite of role overload.

The case of the discharge nurse

Theresa Jones is the Ward Manager of a very busy ward. She is seen as being competent and is well liked by her colleagues.

The Trust decides to implement the idea of having a nurse who is solely concerned with the discharge of patients from the hospital to try and expedite the discharge process. Analysis had shown that many patients are staying in hospital longer than is strictly necessary because of, for example, the 'timing' of medical ward rounds, problems in the patients' homes, lack of support in the community and so on.

Theresa Jones is delighted by this opportunity and relishes the prospect of increasing the efficiency of the Trust overall. However, she soon runs into major problems with the consultants, who refuse to have anything to do with her and will not allow her to question their decisions about discharges. She also finds Social Services is absolutely intransigent, arguing that it has no more resources to put into any developments in community care.

Theresa Jones soon finds that the job is a non-job. She is blocked at every turn. Her expectations of a challenging job disappear like puffs of smoke and she becomes disenchanted and miserable with herself and her colleagues.

A number of attempts are made to try and steer her in 'the right direction', but none of these succeed. Theresa Jones starts to moan and carp about the lack of cooperation from just about everybody, including her old colleagues – she becomes a difficult person.

In essence, Theresa believes that there is little she can do. She is suffering from role underload created, in part, by the different expectations of the role she herself has and those the people whose cooperation she needs have.

An analysis of Theresa Jones' situation, comparing her expectations of the job with what has actually happened, immediately shows where the problems are. Consequently, the job is redesigned to give Theresa more scope for deploying her own ideas and, from this, she is able to build it up into a successful part of the running of the ward – planning the discharge of patients even before they have been admitted to hospital. Incidentally, Theresa uses the negotiating tool to persuade the recalcitrant doctors that it is in their interests to streamline the discharge process.

Role overlap

Role overlap often occurs because of role ambiguity. Here two roles seem to have similar sorts of responsibilities and there is constant debate between the role holders as to who should do what. Role overlap can sometimes occur between managers and subordinates where the manager is perceived by the subordinate as intruding on their territory. Such situations can give rise to considerable conflict and disagreements, with much unhappiness on the part of both role holders.

A way out of this is for the parties to come together and negotiate the boundaries of their roles. 'I will do this, if you will do that' is the sort of discussion that might be had. The important thing is that the cause of the problem is not necessarily a personality clash, but just the result of roles being ill defined and overlapping and that nobody has sat down to work out how they can work together in greater harmony. Take the case of Tony – a junior in CSSD.

CSSD and Tony

After five years of a constant level of staffing, one member of the six-strong team in the CSSD has left. The gap is filled by Tony, a younger member of staff than the others.

It had been anticipated that Tony's role would be a junior one because the group has a woolly hierarchy, and a junior employee is desperately needed so there will be someone to do the less demanding tasks. For the first three months, this works very well – the three older women in the team rather enjoy having a 'young man' around, and Tony soon finds that he has their support on many of the issues discussed.

The Team Manager, Jock Staples, notices how well Tony is doing, especially working with the three older women. He asks Tony to take on more responsible work. Soon, though, problems begin to occur. John and Petra, the other two team members are not happy as Tony begins to intrude on their territory. He takes calls from the ward staff and theatres that are intended for them and, when challenged, Tony replies, 'Surely it does not matter who does it – just as long as it is done'. The problem is exacerbated when Jock praises Tony for his initiative and holds him up as an example to the others.

Cooperation over work matters breaks down completely as first John and then Petra begin to complain about Tony's intrusion into their work and areas of responsibility.

Several weeks go by, with confusion reigning in the group as the older women have no desire to alienate John and Petra, with whom they have worked for five years, but they cannot turn on Tony, whose behaviour is becoming difficult for them to accept as well.

Tony's work is good and he shows a genuine interest in it. He is friendly to all his colleagues and has invited all of them to a barbecue in the summer (although John and Petra have declined to go). Something urgently needs doing, however, to repair the divisions in the group before work standards fall or a valuable member of staff is lost.

Fortunately, Jock has become aware of the problem before it is too late and brings everyone together round a table to examine the various roles and relationships and agree boundaries.

Using the Role Analysis Tool

Role analysis is useful for analysing causes of difficult behaviour. The symptoms of such behaviour can be stress, anxiety, lack of cooperation and all the other syndromes associated with difficult people. Once you can be analytical about the potential causes of difficult behaviour and see them in terms of their relation to roles, this enables you to start to sort out with individuals the boundaries of their roles, ways of resolving conflicts within their roles, clarifying areas of ambiguity and so on. Once role-related problems are recognized, their resolution depends on open communication, a willingness to negotiate changes, but also a recognition of the fact that role-related problems rarely disappear altogether in fast-changing organizations. There is a need for constant surveillance of this aspect and a willingness to negotiate changes.

By using the Role analysis worksheet shown below, you can work out whether or not the difficult behaviour you are concerned about is caused by role-related problems. Use it as an *aide-mémoire* to define the role problem and develop options for its resolution. You could use the worksheet on your own or as an agenda item for a discussion with your colleagues.

Role analysis worksheet

1. Is the problem role-related?

   ☐ Yes   ☐ No

2. If 'Yes', what dimension of the role leads to difficulties and what evidence do you have of this?

3. How can you test your analysis?

4. What changes in the role could you make to resolve these difficulties?

5. How will you go about making the requisite changes?

Chapter 13

The Values Tool

Values and beliefs are fundamental assumptions that people hold about their work, their lives and how they should behave in relation to others and themselves. It is not often that people think deeply about the values and beliefs that are influencing their behaviour. They are assumed, and so each person tends to assume that everybody else shares those values as well. This clearly is not the case. People have different sets of values and base their behaviour on these. These values determine what, for them, is important in life and what is not important. People are often accused of difficult behaviour when it is their values and beliefs that are governing their reactions to circumstances.

An extreme example would be those Catholics who will not be involved in abortions. Some may see these staff as 'being difficult'; others would argue that their values should be respected.

Examples of values or beliefs that people may hold are the following:

'A doctor should always do the best for a patient irrespective of cost.'
'Medicine should always prolong life.'
'Organizations should be based on boss/subordinate relationships.'
'Patients should be treated as individuals.'
'Honesty is always the best policy.'
'Healthcare should never be rationed.'

You may find it hard to disagree with any of these, but some people do act as if they do. You can readily see that some of these values are bound to create conflict. For example, a consultant rheumatologist was alleged to have shortened his patient's life by administering a particular dosage of a drug. A nurse concerned with looking after this patient believed the consultant had been involved in a 'mercy' killing, which, in terms of her values, was wrong. In her view, the consultant was acting contrary to one of the most strongly held medical values – that a doctor should not deliberately shorten another person's life. The nurse informed the authorities and the consultant was eventually charged with murder. He was found not guilty. This case shows very clearly a clash of values and, as such, aroused powerful feelings in those involved. Some argued strongly that the nurse should have kept quiet, but for her, and many others, her values 'forced' her to report the matter.

Turning to another important but not such a life-threatening issue, consider the case of a female Personnel Director who is a member of the Trust's Executive Board. The Board tends to organize its meetings beginning late in the afternoon and often running through into the early or late evening. This happens at least twice a month. This causes the Personnel Director great difficulty because she has a family to attend to and for her – although her work is extremely important – the values are that the integrity of her family is more important than work.

By raising this problem with the Board, it was agreed that the meetings of the Board would be held earlier, and the fact that the Personnel Director left the hospital at 5 o'clock was no longer considered as 'sloping off early'. Even so, some Board members' values put work first and family second and so they argued that if this was unacceptable to the Personnel Director, then she should leave. It is sometimes difficult for people to accept values that are different to their own. It is often pointless to argue about values because they are so embedded in a person's belief system that rational argument is unlikely to change them.

Of course, values can be used as an excuse for obstinacy. This happens when the values are not really believed in but are proffered as an excuse for not doing something. For example, Tim Smith is a young accounts clerk who lives with his elderly parents. He points out many times to his colleagues that it his view that he should support his parents and so he must get home at a reasonable hour to prepare meals for them.

Everyone is impressed by Tim's commitment to his parents and is quite happy to relieve him of some work so that he can fulfil this commitment fully. It is only when Tim is found to be going to football matches and not looking after his parents at all that everyone realizes that Tim has been 'pulling a fast one', as the saying goes.

If you suspect that the cause of 'difficulties' and a 'difficult' person is a clash of values, you might find it useful to complete the Value Clarification worksheet below and invite the other person to do the same. Alternatively, if you can be more precise about the actual value that is causing you difficulties, arrange to meet informally to discuss with the 'difficult' person what you and they really believe is important. Once you have each understood the differences in importance that you attach to various behaviours or attitudes, you can construct a way of working together that reduces the number of occasions when your values come into conflict. The most important approach, as you will see, is being able to talk relatively objectively about those things that you believe passionately in. This is where some of the communication skills discussed earlier will come into play. It is especially important for you to be able to paraphrase (see page 50) back to the other person what you perceive to be their values and encourage them to do the same for you so that you come to a genuine understanding of each other's values and beliefs. Only in this way will you begin to build together a genuine way of working that will avoid difficulties in the future.

Value clarification worksheet

Aim

The aim of this worksheet is to help you identify your values and compare these with the values of others. If you can complete this exercise together with the 'difficult' person, you will gain real understanding of each other.

The process

Step 1
You and the 'difficult' person write a sentence in response to each of the questions in Section 1 (below).

Step 2
You and the other person list your key values.

Step 3
Each identify potential conflict areas and consider how you can develop a way of living together.

Section 1: Value clarification worksheet

What values govern your behaviour with regard to the following areas?

Areas	Your response	Other's response
Relating to family		
Relating to work subordinates		
Relating to work superiors		
Relating to strangers		
Work itself and objectives		
Leisure time		
Illegal acts of others		
Acts of others contrary to your values		
Health		

Infringements on your
liberty by others

Infringements on your
health by others

Working for your
organization

Charitable work or
donation to charities

Section 2: Value clarification worksheet

From your analysis of the answers to Section 1, what conclusions do you draw about the five to eight most important values for yourself and the other person? Please write them down in the table below.

Your values	Other's values
1.	
2.	
3.	
4.	
5.	
6.	
7.	
8.	

Section 3: Value clarification worksheet

Please consider and write down what the differences between your values and those of the other are. Is there conflict?

If there is conflict, how will you raise this with the other person and develop an approach that means you can work together respecting/acknowledging the values of the other?

14

The Power Tool

If you will excuse the pun, the power tool is intended to be used to construct a base of power and influence from which you can deal more easily with those difficult people. The power tool is an investment strategy and, as with many investments, it takes a little time before you can reap the full dividends.

In an organization such as a hospital, there are not many occasions when traditional sources of power work well. By this is meant that authoritarian rule is no longer an acceptable way, to most people, of being managed. It might have been acceptable in the days when Simon Sparrow was a young house officer and Sir Lancelot Spratt was able to 'lord' it over just about everyone, but, these days, naked power is just not acceptable. Even when someone is in a senior position, such as a chief executive, the use of power should be kept for extreme circumstances only. Even then, when using it, a wise chief executive makes sure that they have the support of others before exercising authoritarian power.

What is power? Power is the ability to get things done in a way that you would wish. In dealing with 'difficult' people, power can be used to influence or persuade them to change their behaviour. The power tool is an investment strategy because it aims to build up (in the eyes of people who may cause you problems in the future) a perception of you as being someone who is able to exercise power – that is, someone who can 'get things done'.

As with any other investment strategy, the power tool can be misused. If you attempt to build up a base of power and you then exercise that power with a lack of integrity – you play games with people and try to manipulate them – you will be found out and your source of power will disappear. So, one important aspect of using the power tool is to behave with integrity in dealing with people and not try to score points for the sake of showing how 'powerful' you are.

Key skills in the use of the power tool are those of being able to:

- diagnose a situation and understand what is happening
- recognize who has the decision-making authority and who else is associated with the decision-making process.

For example, with regard to the latter, it is very well known that personal assistants to chief executives and others are, despite their relatively lowly position in the hierarchy of the organization, extremely influential because they guard access to the 'boss'.

In addition to these two critical aspects of being able to recognize when it is necessary to use it and then act with integrity, there are other aspects of power that you can capitalize on. First, there is what is called 'expert power', where your knowledge and skills in a particular subject area are acknowledged to be expert. As such, your words will be listened to and you will be able to persuade those people who acknowledge your expertise to change.

Another source of power is 'reference power'. In this case, your power is drawn from those you associate with who are well respected in the organization. Extending this a little further, those who build networks of contacts are influential because they may know somebody who is either expert or recognized as being 'powerful' in other ways in the organization.

To help you assess where you are in terms of your power investment strategy, a series of questions has been devised – the Power worksheets; see pages 112–121 – to test your knowledge, expertise, behaviour in support of others and diagnostic skills. The questions are based on the results of research into what makes those who are perceived to be powerful in organizations have that power. Try to answer the questions truthfully because the results will then pinpoint accurately where you are in the power stakes. Remember that the questions where your score may be low can direct you as to what sorts of actions you might take to increase the level of power that you have.

Once you have developed your sources of power, you will find it much easier to deal with difficult people. Note, though, that this will occur not as a result of overtly exercising your power, but, rather, because others recognize that you could do so if you needed to. In other words, the skilled user of the power tool does not need to demonstrate their power: it is sufficient that others know they have power.

Let's take the case of Ian before moving on to complete the Power worksheets.

Ian builds his power base

Ian is Public Relations Manager for an acute Trust. He is good at his job – in other words he has 'expert' power. Not only this, but, over the years, he has built up a network of colleagues both inside and outside the Trust. By using this network, and by doing favours to people in the network, Ian is alerted to 'problems' before they hit the fan. Quite often, he can prevent a problem becoming embarrassing to the Trust by 'negotiating' deals with his colleagues in the network – particularly journalists.

Ian has also built up his 'reference' power. He has immediate access to the Chairman and Chief Executive because he makes sure that they are well briefed and prepared when facing public meetings or having to appear on TV programmes.

Very few people are difficult with Ian; he can nearly always achieve the outcomes he wants. Hardly ever, though, does he need to 'trade' on his power sources. He has invested and reaps the dividends. Others know that even though he is not one of the most senior members of staff, he still is able to wield considerable power. However, it has taken time for his investments to provide the dividends that he values. He is also shrewd enough to know that any lack of integrity or abuse of the power connections on his part will 'unplug' the power tool; it will then no longer work.

The Power Worksheets

The aim of the Power worksheets is to give you some insight into your current basis of power. Try to answer the questions accurately. Whenever you score 3 or below, you can reckon on having some 'investment' work to do. In these cases, you will be invited to decide on which investment actions you are going to take.

Power worksheet 1

Questions about your expertise and knowledge

Instructions
Put an X on each of the scales below at the point that represents your view about yourself in a specific situation (such as your job or an outside interest, such as the governing body of a school). Please think carefully before answering and be completely honest.

1. To what extent are you expert in your field?

   1 ——— 2 ——— 3 ——— 4 ——— 5

   To a limited   To the fullest
   extent   extent

2. To what extent is your expertise recognized by those you seek to influence?

   1 ——— 2 ——— 3 ——— 4 ——— 5

   To a limited   To the fullest
   extent   extent

3. To what extent can you claim relevant but indirect expertise?

   1 ——— 2 ——— 3 ——— 4 ——— 5

   To a limited   To the fullest
   extent   extent

4. How extensive is your information network?

   1 ——— 2 ——— 3 ——— 4 ——— 5

   Limited   Very extensive

5. How frequently do you provide unsolicited but relevant information to others?

1 ——————— 2 ——————— 3 ——————— 4 ——————— 5

Infrequently   Frequently

6. How well organized is your information base about others and their requirements/interests/needs?

1 ——————— 2 ——————— 3 ——————— 4 ——————— 5

Non-existent   Well organized

7. How frequently are significant decisions made without your information/ideas/contributions?

1 ——————— 2 ——————— 3 ——————— 4 ——————— 5

Frequently   Infrequently

8. How closely are you perceived to be associated with the organization's objectives, traditions and norms?

1 ——————— 2 ——————— 3 ——————— 4 ——————— 5

Separated   Very closely

9. To what extent are you perceived to be professionally credible?

1 ——————— 2 ——————— 3 ——————— 4 ——————— 5

To a limited   To the fullest
extent   extent

10. To what extent are you known outside your organization but still in your 'professional' field?

1 ——————— 2 ——————— 3 ——————— 4 ——————— 5

To a limited   To the fullest
extent   extent

Scoring

40–50	You have a power base and only need to maintain it.
30–40	You are building your power base, but need to strengthen some aspects – look especially at scales where you have scored 3 and below.
20–30	You need to take action to demonstrate your knowledge and expertise to others or build these up.
10–20	Urgent action is needed to build up your expertise and knowledge.

Now that you have completed your analysis, go back to the scales where your score is 3 or below and specify two actions you will take to build up your power base, then write these down.

Power worksheet 2

Questions about your behaviour

Instructions

Put an X on each of the scales below at the point that represents your view about yourself in a specific situation (such as your job or an outside interest, such as the governing body of a school). Please think carefully before answering and be completely honest.

1. How consistent is your behaviour in relating to all categories and levels of staff?

   1 ——— 2 ——— 3 ——— 4 ——— 5

   Highly inconsistent   Highly consistent

2. How predictable is your behaviour in normal daily circumstances?

   1 ——— 2 ——— 3 ——— 4 ——— 5

   Unpredictable   Very predictable

3. To what extent do you believe that people would share a personal problem with you?

I——————— 2 ——————— 3 ——————— 4 ——————— 5

To no extent   To the fullest
                                                     extent

4. To what extent would your subordinates share a work difficulty with you?

I——————— 2 ——————— 3 ——————— 4 ——————— 5

To no extent   To the fullest
                                                     extent

5. To what extent are perceptions of your trustworthiness based on hard evidence?

I——————— 2 ——————— 3 ——————— 4 ——————— 5

To no extent   To the fullest
                                                     extent

6. To what extent are you perceived as forming your own views/judgements and sticking to them?

I——————— 2 ——————— 3 ——————— 4 ——————— 5

To no extent   To the fullest
                                                     extent

7. To what extent do you enjoy a reputation based on values that most people in your organization would support?

I——————— 2 ——————— 3 ——————— 4 ——————— 5

To no extent   To the fullest
                                                     extent

8. How frequently do people seek your advice and support?

I——————— 2 ——————— 3 ——————— 4 ——————— 5

Infrequently   Frequently

9. How frequently is your advice on non-task-related issues acted on?

    I——————— 2 ——————— 3——————— 4——————— 5

    Infrequently   Frequently

10. To what extent are your people-related decisions based on a careful consideration of their effect on them?

    I——————— 2 ——————— 3——————— 4——————— 5

    To no extent   To the fullest
                                                    extent

Scoring

40–50   You are seen as trustworthy and someone who can be relied on.

30–40   People may be unsure about you and not absolutely confident in you.

20–30   You are not seen as someone of integrity and need to take action on this.

10–20   Your power is severely limited because of how people regard you.

Where you have scored 3 or less on a scale, decide what investment actions you are going to take and write these down.

Power worksheet 3

Questions about your support of others

Instructions
Put an X on each of the scales below at the point that represents your view about yourself in a specific situation (such as your job or an outside interest, such as the governing body of a school). Please think carefully before answering and be completely honest.

1. To what extent do you actively seek out contacts and plan to engage with them?

   1 ———— 2 ———— 3 ———— 4 ———— 5

   To no extent   To the fullest extent

2. To what extent do you make deliberate efforts to keep your network 'live'?

   1 ———— 2 ———— 3 ———— 4 ———— 5

   To no extent   To the fullest extent

3. How frequently do you organize events that can enhance your network?

   1 ———— 2 ———— 3 ———— 4 ———— 5

   Infrequently   Frequently

4. How frequently do you attend events that can enhance your network?

   1 ———— 2 ———— 3 ———— 4 ———— 5

   Infrequently   Frequently

5. To what extent do you build up obligations to yourself?

   1 ———— 2 ———— 3 ———— 4 ———— 5

   To no extent   To the fullest extent

6. If it were possible, to what extent would you rearrange your schedule to do someone a favour?

   1 ———— 2 ———— 3 ———— 4 ———— 5

   To no extent   To the fullest extent

7. To what extent do you take deliberate action to ensure that your own staff support you?

1——————— 2 ——————— 3 ——————— 4 ——————— 5

To no extent   To the fullest
                                          extent

Scoring

30–35	Your network will be, or already is, a considerable source of power to you.
25–30	Being a little more proactive in building and maintaining your network would help.
20–25	You need to begin to build a network.
15–20	You may be seen as a bit of a 'loner' without many friends 'at court'.

Where you have scored 3 or lower on a scale, decide what investment actions you are going to take to increase your power base and write these down.

Power worksheet 4

Questions about your diagnostic skills

Instructions
Put an X on each of the scales below at the point that represents your view about yourself in a specific situation (such as your job or an outside interest, such as the governing body of a school). Please think carefully before answering and be completely honest. In answering the following questions, recall a significant change/project/event that you had to manage and use this as the basis for your responses.

1. To what extent did you map out those individuals whose cooperation would be necessary?

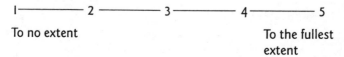

1——————— 2 ——————— 3 ——————— 4 ——————— 5

To no extent   To the fullest
                                          extent

2. To what extent did you deliberately attempt to ascertain their degree of cooperation?

```
1 ———— 2 ———— 3 ———— 4 ———— 5
```

To no extent   To the fullest
                                                extent

3. To what extent did you deliberately identify potential areas of resistance and their causes?

```
1 ———— 2 ———— 3 ———— 4 ———— 5
```

To no extent   To the fullest
                                                extent

4. To what extent did you identify those whose compliance was necessary?

```
1 ———— 2 ———— 3 ———— 4 ———— 5
```

To no extent   To the fullest
                                                extent

5. To what extent did you test whether or not such compliance would be forthcoming?

```
1 ———— 2 ———— 3 ———— 4 ———— 5
```

To no extent   To the fullest
                                                extent

6. To what extent did you try to formulate strategies that would meet the needs and interests of others?

```
1 ———— 2 ———— 3 ———— 4 ———— 5
```

To no extent   To the fullest
                                                extent

7. To what extent did you attempt to assess what levels of dissatisfaction (if any) there were with the present situation?

```
1 ———— 2 ———— 3 ———— 4 ———— 5
```

To no extent   To the fullest
                                                extent

8. To what extent did you test out the commitment to your vision of the future?

I ——————— 2 ——————— 3 ——————— 4 ——————— 5

To no extent   To the fullest extent

9. To what extent did you attempt to assess the costs (social, psychological, economic, financial) of change by others?

I ——————— 2 ——————— 3 ——————— 4 ——————— 5

To no extent   To the fullest extent

10. To what extent did you involve others in developing your plan for change?

I ——————— 2 ——————— 3 ——————— 4 ——————— 5

To no extent   To the fullest extent

Scoring

40–50   Your diagnostic processes are very good.

30–40   You may need to collect more information to ensure your diagnosis is comprehensive in future.

20–30   You need to be thorough and probably systematic in your diagnosis.

10–20   You probably manage change with your fingers crossed.

Where you have scored 3 or lower on any scale, decide what investment actions you are going to take to build up your diagnostic skills.

Once you have completed all the Power worksheets, you should have a number of ideas about where you need to make investments so that you can use the power tool to deliver results in your dealings with 'difficult people' where you are. As suggested, it is extremely useful to write down what investment actions you are going to take under each of the four headings of the worksheets:

- expertise and knowledge
- behaviour
- support of others, which is networking
- diagnostic skills.

Power is most effective when you do not actually need to deploy it. Actually deploying your power can be 'messy', creating battles and animosities, hence the stress placed on the investment nature of the power tool.

The aim, therefore, is to develop a power base such that the difficult person recognizes that they must change their behaviour otherwise you have the 'power' to make life uncomfortable for them. It is the potential of your power that is most effective and the recognition of this on the part of others.

Chapter 15

The Stress Management Tool

We now come to the penultimate 'tool' for handling difficult people. The basis for this tool is that some difficult behaviour is caused by stress that is being experienced by the 'difficult' persons themselves. Such stress can be created by any number of factors, such as changing jobs, new colleagues, difficult work, tight deadlines, personal crises and so on.

It may be that you can do little about these stressors. They exist and they affect the behaviour of the other person. What you may be able to do, though, is help the other person through the stress they are experiencing. To do this, it is helpful to understand how people react to stress and shock. The following approach is based on the bereavement process and does, I think, have applications to other causes of stress.

Stages of Stress

The first stage

This stage is that when the stress or shock starts. At this time, individuals can feel panicky and uncertain, not be able to sort things out in their own mind and believe that their world has collapsed about them.

It is almost impossible to think and plan coherently when in this stage, so the best thing for you to do is just listen and demonstrate that you are attempting to understand the problems they face. Do not start thinking about the future yet.

The second stage

Then comes the stage of 'denial', with attempts being made to carry on as though nothing was changing, but of course things have changed and old behaviours will not work in the new context.

During this stage, and assuming you have built up some rapport with the stressed person, you can very gently raise issues by asking questions – the answers to which demand a recognition that changes have happened. You may need to tolerate anger, bitterness and blaming behaviour when you do this, but, as long as you do not react defensively, you should maintain the relationship.

The third stage

As the stressed individual moves out of the above stage, they will move into the third phase, which is when they acknowledge the need to change and settle down to work out what needs to be done.

Here what is required is the ability to facilitate their thinking and planning processes by means of your listening, questioning and rapport-building skills. During this stage, the stressed individual should have the opportunity to prove to themselves that they can operate successfully in this new environment and to discuss regularly with you how they are coping.

The final stage

In the end, as a result of your supportive actions, the individual should be able to cope with the new context without the stress that was experienced initially, gradually building up their confidence. Of course, reaching this stage can take some time, as the stressed person needs to come to an understanding of the causes of the problems and develop a mechanism to better cope with them.

A note on dealing with stress

This may read as being rather too simple, but it is not the intention here to trivialize a real cause of difficult behaviour – that of stress. Those readers who are skilled helpers may think that insufficient weight has been given to the counselling processes that are involved in helping those who are stressed. They may be right, but I believe that all managers, rather than just the expert ones, should be able to employ the basic skills of listening, developing rapport and providing support to those whose behaviour may be difficult due to stress. Also, having such skills is important because, should it become apparent that the stress experienced is so great that the individual needs professional support, then the manager needs to be able to recognize this and encourage the difficult person to seek such guidance, either through the occupational health service or from some external source.

Analysing Glenda Jones' Problems

If we now return to Glenda Jones, who you will recall meeting at the beginning of this book, you may now know what your diagnosis is and what change levers and tools you might use to achieve the outcomes you will have specified.

In my view, Glenda experienced the inevitable stresses involved in changing jobs and location. Just as when you transplant a plant, you prepare both the plant and the ground for the change, so you must prepare an individual for change. If you don't do this in the case of a plant, it will die. In the case of an individual, lack of preparation will produce problem behaviours.

You may believe that there was some role ambiguity in Glenda's job and that if time had been taken to clarify this with her staff and her manager it would have been worth while. As her time with the new Trust passed and she became more unhappy, and probably more 'difficult', so her motivation would have changed – in fact, it had all but evaporated (she did leave, after all). To restore this, and a positive approach to the job, many of the tools described would need to be used.

It is apparent, though, that had others been more aware of the early stages of her unhappiness – or helped her manage the transition into the new job – she would never have become 'difficult' at all. As was said at the beginning of the book, all behaviour is rationalized – our job is to detect this rationale and, thereby, better understand the causes of difficult behaviour earlier rather than later. In this way, we may be able to prevent difficulties in the future by taking positive and supportive action now. For example, stress is sometimes occasioned by people feeling negative in some way about their work. In these cases, just dealing with the symptoms is inadequate – you have to identify the causes of the stress.

Consider the case of Sarah who, with Maria, is working on a project to speed up 'patient flows' through the Accident and Emergency and Out-patients Departments – it is a mini re-engineering project.

The case of 'stressed Sarah'

Sarah has always worked in a team; her strongest point on her CV is her 'adaptability' to working with new people and her determination to understand them. However, as a result of the current economy drive, many of her colleagues were made redundant or moved to other departments, leaving Sarah in a team of just two – herself and Maria. To be fair, the workload has diminished, too, with most of the spadework having been delegated to other departments or now speeded up by the new computer-driven office. Sarah is keen to learn – she has been sent on several computer courses and has returned from them amazed by what computers can do.

In recent months, however, Sarah's line manager, Sally Jacks, has received complaints from people working on the same floor. (The office is open plan and the desks quite close together as several departments have merged in an attempt to economize. New offices are being sought, but the prognosis for more space in the near future is not good.) Sarah's colleagues say that she appears incapable of working on her own and is constantly on the telephone to her former colleagues asking 'simple or downright stupid' questions about the project she is working on. If not, she is chatting to her project partner.

The strongest complaint has come from Maria, her project partner, who says she cannot concentrate for more than ten minutes without Sarah either asking a question or sighing in frustration if she is trying to work something out and failing. The result has been Maria doing a fair amount of Sarah's work as well as her own, which has entailed her working late, causing tension at home. Maria believes that Sarah is capable of doing the work set, but that she doesn't give herself time or organize things properly and becomes stressed too easily. Sarah has worked on her own success-fully before, but it appears that the last two years working in a team have deprived her of her ability to work alone.

When Sally Jacks mentions all this to Sarah, Sarah replies that personal contact between departments is vital to prevent the organization losing its identity, and that the project is causing difficulties because sufficient information had not been given to her at the outset, which is why she has spent a lot of time 'chasing' other departments. She also hints that although Maria is working more quickly, and quietly, than her, this is not indicative of the quality of her work.

- What diagnosis would you give for this set of problems?
- Are they caused by the changes, leading to increased stress in Sarah because she is more exposed in a small section?
- Is it a competency problem or a self-efficacy issue?
- Motivation seems all right – but is it?
- Have the changes altered roles, which are proving ill defined or leading to overload?

As with all cases of difficult behaviour, here is a set of overlapping issues that need careful thought in order to produce a clear spec-ification of outcomes and select the right levers and tools to restore Sarah's 'usual' approach to work. What would you do?

Chapter 16

Difficult People and Their Grievances

'Difficult' people frequently see others as being the 'difficult' ones. They may blame everyone else and everything else for the problems. This can make it extremely difficult in dealing with them, especially as it is likely that you do not share or believe their allegations. Their very unreasonableness, as you experience it, can make you angry and frustrated. Yet, you have to deal with what they say properly and fairly because if you don't you give your difficult person yet another excuse or reason for their difficult behaviour – namely, you!

In these circumstances, when your difficult person is raising a grievance about others, it is very useful to have a practical step-by-step process to follow. This enables you to keep control and provides a systematic basis for managing the encounter. Such a process is set out below.

The Six-step Process for Handling a 'Grievance'

Before you begin, decide where you want any discussion to take place. Ideally it should be in private, without the possibility of interruption. Be prepared to take notes.

Step 1: Clear the air

The other person will probably be feeling uptight and so in this first step, your task is to let them vent their frustrations. Listen to what they say, check your understanding of it by paraphrasing (see pages 50–52) and make notes of the points they make. Encourage them to get it all off their chest. You need to understand the length and breadth of their grievance, however unjustified you may think it is. Don't argue, defend or seek to justify at this stage. Interrupt only to achieve greater clarification or to paraphrase.

Be careful not to come to pre-formed judgements; demonstrate your openness and willingness to listen by asking questions of clarification. When you think the other has finished, refer to your notes and summarize the grievances they have, asking at the end if your understanding is both accurate and complete. Once you have agreement to this, you can move on to the next step.

Step 2: Probing for reasons

In this step, you are trying to get behind the presenting symptoms to find reasons for them. The best way to do this is to ask the other person a series of questions. These questions concern the context and circumstances surrounding the grievance, as well as their ideas about causes and effects. For example, is there anything in the other's behaviour that causes a disagreeable effect? You are likely to elicit defensive responses to this, but at least you are planting seeds in the mind of the other.

At this stage, questions beginning with 'Why. . .?', 'Where. . .?', 'When. . .?', 'How. . .?' and 'What. . .?' will be the most productive.

At the conclusion of this stage, summarize what you now understand to be the potential causes of the grievance, then explain that you will now need to investigate these and say how you will go about this. Check that this is acceptable to the other person and if it is not, ask why. This may identify other issues that have not so far been revealed.

Step 3: The investigation

At this stage, you need the facts. Plan who you will see, what you will ask them, what documents (such as job descriptions) you need, and so on. Find out if there have been any changes that might have been a prelude to the grievance.

Step 4: Come to a decision

At this point, you must be at your most open-minded and fair. You have to decide whether or not the grievance has any foundation. If it does, what the cause and effect chain is and whether or not the 'aggrieved' party is themselves part of the cause. If so, how you are going to explain this so that you effect a change in their behaviour. Also, if anyone else needs to change and how you are going to achieve the necessary changes.

Step 5: Giving your judgement

You will meet again with the aggrieved person. In this session, you will be doing the talking. Explain how you have investigated the grievance, making sure not to betray any confidences, then describe what you have found.

Next, explain your decision and what you intend to do to implement it. If the aggrieved person needs to change, you may wish to select one of the tools described earlier to bring about the change – a typical tool to use in these circumstances is that of negotiation.

Do not allow this session to go over all the old ground of the grievance – explain that you have taken all these aspects into your consideration. If the aggrieved person is still unhappy with the decisions and actions, explain how your formal grievance procedure works and refer them to the next stage.

Assuming they will accept your decision, check that they fully understand this by asking them to summarize it to you. After this, explain that you will be reviewing how the changes are working in an agreed number of weeks' time.

Step 6: The review

Review when you said you would by discussing with all those involved whether or not any changes have occurred. If they have, breathe a sigh of relief. If they have not, you will need to investigate why not and decide what tool you will now use to gain compliance to your decision.

Chapter 17

Discipline and Dismissal – The Final Blow

This is the final tool, in more senses than one. It may be that the threat of the tool will be sufficient, but its finality means it must be used with great care.

Quite rightly, the processes of discipline and ultimate dismissal are carefully circumscribed by legislation. After all, you could be depriving someone of their livelihood. This means that if you embark on this process, it must be with the support of your own manager and probably that of appropriate members of a personnel department. They will guide you through their own processes, which will probably have been negotiated with staff representatives.

Disciplining staff is one of the most difficult aspects of any manager's job, but, nevertheless, an important one. If disciplinary action is not taken at the right time, then the rest of the workforce can become disillusioned with the way that management is managing. It is not to be shirked, therefore, if you are convinced that you are at the point where you need to use this tool of last resort.

The Context of Discipline

Disciplinary action is normally the final stage in dealing with difficult people. If a person's performance or behaviour is causing you concern, then you must consider what is causing the behaviour or poor performance. As stressed earlier in the book, you must make a proper diagnosis of the causes of the difficult behaviour. It may be, for example, that the individual is not trained to undertake the work, does not understand what is required of them, has some personal problem of a temporary nature or is feeling discontented because of poor leadership. It is vital that you can demonstrate that you have tried other approaches before adopting this final one.

The Formal Disciplinary Framework

Disciplinary rules

All organizations should have disciplinary rules that define what types of performance and behaviour could give rise to disciplinary action. These rules should be given to all employees when they are appointed to the organization. You need to assess whether or not your difficult person's behaviour can be said to contravene these rules.

Disciplinary procedures

Organizations should also have a clear set of procedures that explains how to take disciplinary action that may ultimately lead to dismissal.

Appeals against action

Just as there are rules and procedures that govern disciplinary action, there will be an appeals procedure that allows the disciplined member of staff to appeal to a higher managerial authority against the action taken by their manager. This is why it is so important that you have the support of your manager before taking any action and the advice of members of your personnel department on following this procedure correctly.

Stages of Discipline

There are three broad stages of disciplining difficult staff. These are as follows.

Stage 1: Counselling

If an employee's behaviour is unacceptable or their performance is below standard, then the first approach to the problem is one of counselling. In doing this you should:

- encourage the employee to talk about their problems and listen to their answers
- help the employee, by means of discussion, to better understand the nature of their problem
- summarize the results of the counselling session and note these down.

Because this is the final tool, you will almost certainly have had discussions with the difficult person already, so now you need to explain to them that all your past efforts to get the person to change their behaviour appear to have been unsuccessful and that you are having to embark on the disciplinary process.

Stage 2: Written warnings

If counselling does not remedy the situation, you should formally call the employee to account for their poor performance or behaviour. Again, you must encourage the other to talk. It may be that in this session you will find out more about their problem and agree with them steps they can take to overcome it. A formal record is normally kept of these decisions, both parties having a copy of it.

It is at this stage that most difficult people will recognize that you really do mean business. In some procedures, there are two stages to the written warning. The first is the first formal written warning, which, if it does not produce results, will be followed by the final written warning.

Stage 3: Dismissal

Ultimately, it may be that the employment contract has to be terminated. This should be done, once again, after an interview with the other person and in accordance with the employment contract that exists between them and the organization.

Serious Offences

Where the behaviour or performance has involved severe miscon-
duct or dangerous behaviour (such as striking a patient or stealing),
it may be that the employee's contract should be summarily
terminated. This would normally be done after suspending the
employee to investigate the problem, then interviewing them and
hearing their side of the case. If all were unconvinced by this, the
person would be dismissed forthwith.

The Disciplinary Interview

The above has set out a few pointers as to what the formal procedure is for disciplining of staff. It is useful for you to have in mind
a clear framework that you can use when undertaking the
disciplinary interview itself. Do not forget that the purpose of the
disciplinary interview is to identify what actions are necessary to
deal with situations where organizational rules or standards have
been broken.

If you suspect that an individual has behaved in such a way as
to warrant disciplinary action, there are several preliminary steps
that have to be taken. These establish the 'gap' between what is
required of the employee and what is actually being done.

Establishing and agreeing the performance gap

Obviously you will need to refer to any document that specifies
what is expected of the difficult person and then compare this with
evidence relating to their current behaviour or performance standards. The more factual and objective you can be at this stage, the
better. Important documents in this context might be:

- any agreed performance standards and objectives
- records of previous discussion about performance or behaviour
- the organization's disciplinary rules
- job description
- evidence from others, including members of the public.

After this, your next task is to discover what the reasons are for the errant behaviour or inadequate achievements against performance standards. You will hold the interview for this, using probing questions and allowing time for the other person to answer.

Discovering the reasons for the gap

It is very easy to jump to wrong conclusions about the reasons for apparent 'misbehaviour'. Your preparation for the interview should thus attempt to discover:

- recent 'history' of the employee's performance and behaviour – if, for example, there is any pattern to the observed transgression
- the personal circumstances of the employee – say, family problems
- what relationships are like with their colleagues
- whether or not there has been any change in the nature of the work to be done.

Eliminating the gap

Essentially, there are two approaches to eliminating the gap, which are:

- agree with the employee a series of actions or performance standards that will balance the organization's requirements with the individual's achievements
- dismiss the employee.

Effecting changes in the employee's behaviour

For a change in the employee's behaviour to occur, the employee must know quite explicitly what is required and they must accept that such requirements are within their competence to achieve.

It is wise – and often stated as being necessary in disciplinary procedures – that such requirements are written down and sent to the employee, who is asked to acknowledge their receipt; a copy is also put in their file.

It is also quite usual for the employee to be able to appeal against such disciplinary action, and this right must also be conveyed to the employee.

Finally, you will build into this plan for eliminating the gap, a time when progress will be reviewed.

Dismissing the employee

If you decide that dismissal is the only solution, before you embark on this course check that:

- you have the power to dismiss – this should be stated in your disciplinary procedures
- you have conducted the disciplinary interview fairly and in accordance with any agreed procedures
- you do not need to consult any other manager or your personnel department – you almost certainly will have to
- all the proper stages of your disciplinary procedure have been followed and the outcome of each has been properly recorded
- your letter dismissing the employee sets out the reasons for their dismissal and the rights of appeal that they have, and check how this letter should be sent (usually by recorded delivery).

After the Interview

When you have finished the interview, it is vitally important that you record a synopsis of what transpired and what warning, if any, was given.

You should also check your disciplinary procedures to see what the destination of your record and warning should be. At the minimum:

- the employee should receive the warning and acknowledge such receipt (assuming that the disciplinary interview is not just the early counselling session)
- the record and warning should be placed in the employee's personal file
- you should keep a copy of the record and warning as well.

Most procedures allow warnings to be removed after a certain period of proper behaviour. You will wish to make note of this so that you can take the appropriate action at the right time.

A Final Note

As mentioned at the beginning of this chapter, disciplining staff is never an easy matter, but the ideas set out here should enable you to deal with disciplinary problems without causing embarrassment or difficulties and, in particular, achieve changes in the other's performance or behaviour.

As the final tool, it is absolutely essential that all that you do is in accordance with the legislation and rules of your own organization.

Many managers fear the disciplinary process, arguing that 'you can never get rid of staff anyway'. This is not the case, and it is unfair on other staff to have to work with a person who is being difficult and contributing negatively or minimally to the work. However, the importance of dismissal to the difficult person concerned does mean that it should be handled correctly and fairly.

Chapter 18

Conclusion

There is always a reason for people behaving as they do. In dealing with such people, the first step is to try and discover the reason. Sometimes the difficult person will be very clear about why they are behaving as they are, but, more frequently, they will have problems trying to discover why they are doing what they are doing.

Your first job is to fathom the real causes of the difficult behaviour. To do this, you need to understand the other person as much as possible. What makes them tick? When does the difficult behaviour occur? What's in it for them in behaving in this way? Is the person difficult with everyone? Answers to these questions can come from your research, questions, observations and discussions with others.

When President Kennedy was having to deal with what seemed an erratic and angry Nikita Kruschev over the crisis of the missiles in Cuba, Kennedy's research was so thorough that he probably knew Kruschev better than Kruschev knew himself. He knew his life story, what his values were, who his colleagues were and what they expected of him, and, probably, what he had for breakfast!

By understanding the person, you are better able to consider the reason for their outbursts and, just as importantly, the likely reaction to any initiative that might be taken. Preparation, therefore, is vital. Once you have an understanding of the person (the force field analysis tool is a way of aiding you in making a diagnosis), your next step – one frequently overlooked – is to be clear about the outcomes you want to achieve. If you don't know what you are aiming for, then your selection of tools will be quite arbitrary. Don't be over ambitious in setting your desired outcomes. Changing a difficult person's behaviour may take time and if you expect a dramatic 'improvement', you will probably be disappointed.

It has been emphasized that there may well be many symptoms as well as causes of the difficult behaviour. Your task is to try and sort these out by getting down to the 'base problem'. You may need to make a number of attempts at doing this, but don't be disheartened. Eventually, you will unearth the real issues and then be able to select the right tool to remedy the difficulties, which is infinitely better than rushing in with the wrong one.

A final tip. Try to avoid becoming entangled in an emotional web of accusations and blame. When you sense that this may be happening, first, try to paraphrase what the other person is saying to you to calm the process down. If you can't do this, remove yourself from the bear pit. You can do this physically, of course, by leaving, but this is giving up too easily. Instead, play a psychological game by imagining yourself 'in the balcony', observing yourself and the difficult person arguing down below. Creating such psychological distance will enable you to decide how to control the discussion in a cool and collected manner. Sounds strange, but it works.

Feedback from my seminars shows that the tools do work and have encouraged people to have another, more systematic 'go' at resolving the difficulties occasioned by a staff member after having given up when previous attempts had failed.

One of the objectives of this book has been to provide you with the confidence to deal with difficult behaviour. It is when you don't know what to do next, when you are at your wit's end, that feelings of uncertainty and helplessness arise. In this state, you cannot hope to deal with your difficult person. Now you have an approach and a wide range of tools that you can use. They will give you both confidence and competence in dealing with truculent members of staff.

The Robin Gourlay Partnership, which I head runs many programmes on managing and motivating people, including team-building, counselling, appraising performance and so on. We specialize in healthcare work and, should you want to discuss ideas from this book in relation to running courses in your own Trust, you can contact us at:

28 North End
Hursley
Winchester SO21 2JW

Tel: 01962 775569

Further Reading

If you would like to explore some of the ideas in this book a bit further you will find the following both interesting and of practical benefit.

Outcomes

Laborde, G (1987) *Influencing with Integrity*, Syntony, Redwood, CA. Describes the process of defining outcomes and how to evaluate whether they have been achieved.

Communication and Rapport

You will also find some useful ideas on communications and rapport building in Laborde's book. Brooks, M (1990) *Instant Rapport*, Warner Books, Waltham, MA. Includes some useful techniques for building rapport quickly. Schein, E (1969) *Process Consultation Volume 1*, Addison-Wesley, Reading, MA. Explores in more depth some of the processes of interpersonal communication and behaviour.

Luft, J *Of Human Interaction*, National Press Books. Describes in more detail the concept of Johari's window.

Temperaments

Keirsey, D and Bates, M (1984) *Please Understand Me* Prometheus Nemesis UK. An excellent introduction to the Myers-Briggs Type

Indicator. Bayne, R (1995) *The Myers-Briggs Type Indicator – A Critical Review and Practical Guide*. Chapman and Hall, London. A more profound review and practical.

Motivation

Lawler, E *Pay and Organization Development*, Addison-Wesley, Reading, MA. A discussion of Expectancy Theory.
Zimbardo, P and Ebbesen, E *Influencing Attitudes and Changing Behaviour*, Addison-Wesley, Reading MA. Covers a lot of 'motivational ground' and contains a very brief discussion on Re-inforcement Theory. It is a useful read if you wish to explore some motivational theories (eg cognitive dissonance) in more depth.

Negotiations

Fisher, R and Ury, W (1991) *Getting to Yes*, Penguin, London.
Fisher, R and Brown, S *Getting Together*, Hutchinson, London.
Gourlay, R (1987) *Negotiations for Managers*, Mercia Publications, University of Keele. Also takes the ideas further forward.

Power

Greiner, L and Schein, V (1988) *Power and Organization Development – Mobilizing Power to Implement Change*, Addison-Wesley, Reading, MA. Provides a useful analysis of sources of power and thereby how to build it for yourself.

Change

Bridges, W (1996) *Job Shift*, Nicholas Brearley, Princes Risborough, Bucks. Organization changes can be stressful and lead to aberrant behaviour. Contains some practical ideas on preventing and/or coping with this problem.

Roles

Handy, C (1993) *Understanding Organisations*, Penguin, London. A very comprehensive and analytical view on the phenomenon of roles.

Approaches

Goleman, D (1996) *Emotional Intelligence* Bloomsbury, London. Finally, a general book that will encourage you to tackle your difficult people. I have no doubt that this book will open your eyes to the issues involved and encourage you to tackle them as you gain insight into yourself.

Index